1,001 F, ABOUT
PITCHERS

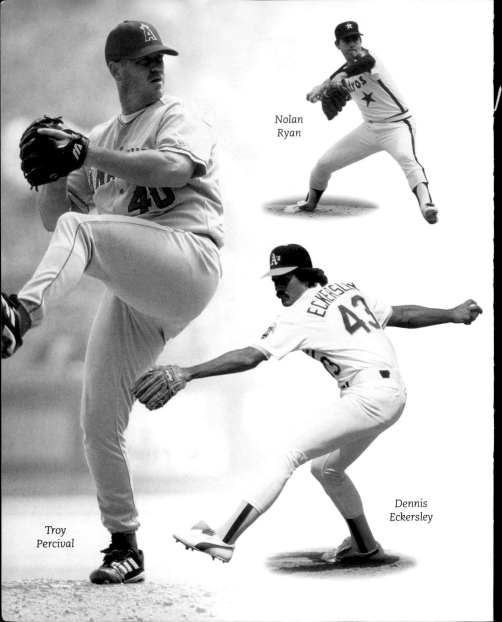

Nolan Ryan

Dennis Eckersley

Troy Percival

MAJOR LEAGUE BASEBALL

1,001 FACTS ABOUT PITCHERS

Mariano
Rivera

By Jim Gigliotti
Statistics Section Compiled By Matt Marini

DK Publishing, Inc.

LONDON, NEW YORK, MELBOURNE,
MUNICH, AND DELHI

Senior Editor Beth Sutinis
Senior Art Editor Michelle Baxter
Publisher Chuck Lang
Creative Director Tina Vaughan
Production Chris Avgherinos

Produced by
Shoreline Publishing Group LLC
Editorial Director James Buckley, Jr.
Art Director Tom Carling, Carling Design, Inc.

Produced in partnership and licensed by Major League Baseball Properties, Inc.
Vice President of Publishing Don Hintze

First American Edition, 2004
04 05 06 07 08 10 9 8 7 6 5 4 3 2 1

Published in the United States by DK Publishing, Inc.
375 Hudson Street, New York, New York 10014

A catalog record for this book is available from the Library of Congress.

ISBN 0-7566-0493-1

DK Publishing books are available at special discounts for bulk purchases for sales promotions or premiums.
Special editions, including personalized covers, excerpts of existing guides, and corporate imprints can be
created in large quantities for specific needs. For more information, contact Special Markets Dept./
DK Publishing, Inc./375 Hudson Street/New York, New York 10014/FAX: 800-600-9098.

Color reproduction by Colourscan, Singapore
Printed in Singapore by Star Standard

Discover more at
www.dk.com

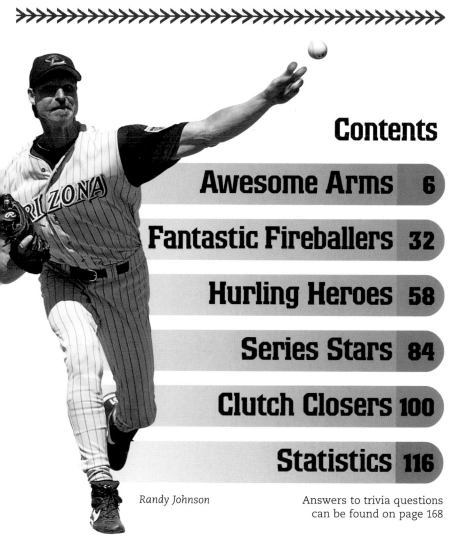

Contents

Randy Johnson

Answers to trivia questions can be found on page 168

Awesome Arms

THEY DON'T ALL BLOW HITTERS AWAY. THEY DON'T ALL SCARE HITTERS. ALL THESE GUYS DO IS WIN...AND WIN...AND WIN.

In 1999, David Cone threw the most recent perfect game, a 4–0 victory over the Expos.

David Cone

THROWS: Righthanded   **MLB CAREER: 1986–2003**

Shortly before the 1987 season opened, the New York Mets obtained 24-year-old pitcher David Cone from Kansas City as part of a five-player trade of mostly little-known players. It turned out to be an enormously one-sided deal in the Mets' favor. David was a part-time starter in 1987, then moved into the rotation in 1988, when he forged a stellar 20-3 record with a 2.22 ERA for the N.L. East champs. He added 14 more wins in each of the next three years. David went on to win 194 games for various clubs in his career. He returned to Kansas City in 1994 and won the Cy Young Award after going 16-5. While with the Yankees in 1999, he pitched a perfect game against Montreal.

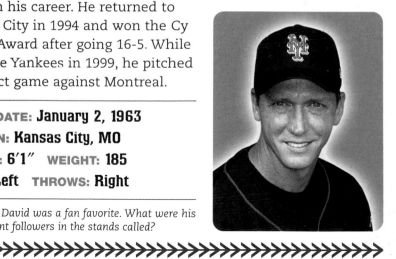

BIRTH DATE: January 2, 1963
BORN IN: Kansas City, MO
HEIGHT: 6'1"   **WEIGHT: 185**
BATS: Left   **THROWS: Right**

TRIVIA: *David was a fan favorite. What were his most ardent followers in the stands called?*

>>

Tom Glavine

THROWS: Lefthanded   **MLB CAREER: 1987–**

Talk about a crafty lefthander and the image of Tom Glavine immediately comes to mind. Though hardly overpowering, Tom has created a highly successful career by mixing speeds and moving location in and out of the strike zone, by fielding his position well, and helping himself at the plate. Glavine, who spent his first 16 big-league seasons in Atlanta before signing with the New York Mets in 2003, had his breakthrough year in 1991, when he won 20 games and earned the first of his two Cy Young Awards. He was a 20-game winner five times for the Braves, earned eight All-Star selections, and was the MVP of Atlanta's World Series triumph in 1995.

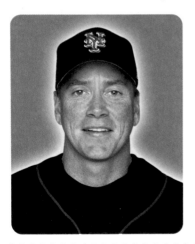

BIRTH DATE: March 25, 1966
BORN IN: Concord, MA
HEIGHT: 6'1"   WEIGHT: 190
BATS: Left   THROWS: Left

TRIVIA: *Tom was drafted in two pro sports. Baseball was one. What was the other?*

>>>

Carl Hubbell

THROWS: Lefthanded   **MLB CAREER: 1928–1943**

While working on a sinker in the minor leagues one day in the mid-1920s, Carl Hubbell unintentionally developed the screwball. It was the pitch that eventually became his "meal ticket"—and earned him that nickname in the big leagues with the New York Giants. Carl won 253 games in 16 seasons, including 115 in a five-year span from 1933–1937. He pitched a no-hitter in 1929, won a record 24 consecutive decisions from 1936–1937, and twice was named the N.L. MVP. He is best known,

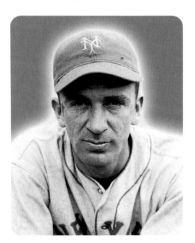

however, for striking out five future Hall of Fame sluggers in a row— Babe Ruth, Lou Gehrig, Jimmie Foxx, Al Simmons, and Joe Cronin—in the 1934 All-Star Game.

BIRTH DATE: June 22, 1903
BORN IN: Carthage, MO
HEIGHT: 6'0"   **WEIGHT: 170**
BATS: Right   **THROWS: Left**

TRIVIA: *In addition to "The Meal Ticket," what was Carl's other nickname?*

Dennis Martinez

THROWS: Righthanded   **MLB CAREER: 1976–1998**

The older Dennis Martinez got, the better he got. After a decade with Baltimore, Dennis was traded to Montreal in 1986. Four years later, at age 35, he was named an All-Star for the first time. The next season, he led the N.L. with an ERA of 2.39 and five shutouts. One of the them was a perfect game against Los Angeles. In seven full seasons with the Expos, he won 97 games and rarely missed a start. Surprisingly, Dennis never won more than 16 games in a season in his career. But he was remarkably consistent, and when he retired in 1998 after one year with Atlanta, his 245 career victories were more than any other Latin American pitcher in Major League history.

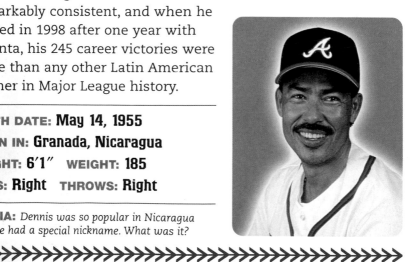

BIRTH DATE: May 14, 1955
BORN IN: Granada, Nicaragua
HEIGHT: 6′1″   **WEIGHT: 185**
BATS: Right   **THROWS: Right**

TRIVIA: *Dennis was so popular in Nicaragua that he had a special nickname. What was it?*

>>>

Pedro Martinez

THROWS: **Righthanded** **MLB CAREER:** **1992–**

He is the first person Red Sox fans want to see on the mound…and the last person most hitters want to see! For more than a decade, Pedro Martinez has been among baseball's top pitchers. With a terrific fastball and a curveball that makes hitters' knees go weak, Pedro has put together some monster seasons. He has not had an ERA higher than 3.00 since 1996. Pedro is one of only three pitchers to win the Cy Young Award in both leagues. He won with Montreal in 1997 and with the Bosox in 1999 and 2000. In 2000, he set an all-time Major League record by holding opponents to a .167 batting average. Pedro broke into the Majors in 1992 with the Dodgers.

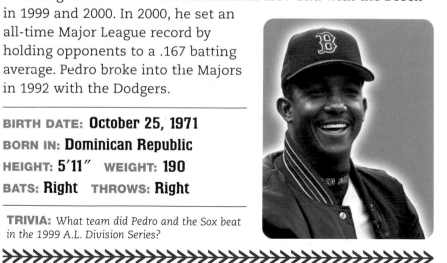

BIRTH DATE: **October 25, 1971**
BORN IN: **Dominican Republic**
HEIGHT: **5'11"**   **WEIGHT:** **190**
BATS: **Right**   **THROWS:** **Right**

TRIVIA: *What team did Pedro and the Sox beat in the 1999 A.L. Division Series?*

>>

Mark Mulder

THROWS: Lefthanded   **MLB CAREER: 2000–**

With Mark Mulder, Tim Hudson, and Barry Zito on their roster, the Oakland A's boast a trio of the most talented arms in baseball today. Mark, the A's top draft pick in 1998, quickly earned a spot in the big club's starting rotation for the 2000 season. He won nine games in 27 starts that year, then really blossomed in 2001, going 21-8 with a 3.45 ERA while tossing a Major League-leading four shutouts. He was second to the Yankees' Roger Clemens in balloting for the A.L. Cy Young Award. Mark then proved that his 2001 season was no fluke when went 19-7 the following year. He had 15 wins in 2003 before going on the diabled list in August.

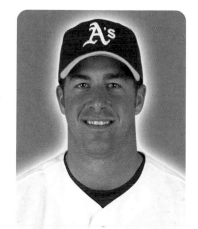

BIRTH DATE: August 5, 1977
BORN IN: South Holland, IL
HEIGHT: 6′6″   WEIGHT: 215
BATS: Left   THROWS: Left

TRIVIA: In 2001, Mark became the third Oakland lefty to win 20 games. Who were the first two?

Mike Mussina

THROWS: Righthanded **MLB CAREER: 1991–**

From 1991–2000, Mike Mussina worked out of the spotlight in Baltimore for a club that reached the postseason just twice. Then he signed with the Yankees in 2001 and has pitched into October every year since. Mike burst onto the scene by going 18-5 with an ERA of 2.54 in 1992, his first full season in the big leagues. He struck out a modest 130 batters that year, but eventually fanned as many as 218 hitters in 1997. After winning 147 games in 10 years with the Orioles, Mike averaged more than 17 victories in his first three seasons in the Bronx. He's come very close to a perfect game three times in his career, once losing his bid on a two-out, two-strike hit in the ninth.

BIRTH DATE: December 8, 1968
BORN IN: Williamsport, PA
HEIGHT: 6′2″ WEIGHT: 185
BATS: Left THROWS: Right

TRIVIA: *Who spoiled Mike's bid for a perfect game with two outs in the ninth in 2001?*

>>>

Hideo Nomo

THROWS: Righthanded   **MLB CAREER: 1995–**

With his distinctive corkscrew windup, Hideo Nomo was dubbed the "Tornado" when he began pitching professionally in Japan. In 1995, the Tornado took the big leagues by storm when he joined the Los Angeles Dodgers and spawned "Nomomania." The Japanese import won 13 games for the Dodgers in 1995 while striking out 236 batters in 191.1 innings and sporting an ERA of 2.54. The next season he won 16 games, among them a no-hitter at Colorado, and struck out 234. Hideo pitched for four other teams—including Boston, where he tossed another no-hitter in 2001—before returning to Los Angeles and winning 16 games again in 2002.

BIRTH DATE: August 31, 1968
BORN IN: Osaka, Japan
HEIGHT: 6'2"   WEIGHT: 210
BATS: Right   THROWS: Right

TRIVIA: *Hideo is one of only four pitchers to toss no-hitters in the A.L. and N.L. Who are the others?*

Jim Palmer

THROWS: Righthanded   **MLB CAREER: 1965–1984**

Jim Palmer was the dominant pitcher on one of the A.L.'s dominant teams of the 1970s, the Baltimore Orioles. From 1970–1978, Jim won 20 or more games eight times and earned three Cy Young Awards. After overcoming arm troubles early in his career, he proved to be remarkably durable by logging more than 300 innings four times in the decade. Jim debuted with the Orioles in 1965, and, at 20 years old in 1966, became the youngest pitcher in World Series history to toss a complete-game shutout.

He went on to cement his reputation as a big-game pitcher by going 8-3 in the postseason. He is the only pitcher to win World Series games in three decades ('60s, '70s, and '80s).

BIRTH DATE: October 15, 1945
BORN IN: New York, NY
HEIGHT: 6'3"   WEIGHT: 196
BATS: Right   THROWS: Right

TRIVIA: *Name the only pitcher in A.L. history with more 20-win seasons than Jim's eight.*

≫≫≫≫≫≫≫≫≫≫≫≫≫≫≫≫≫≫≫≫≫≫≫≫≫≫≫≫≫≫≫≫≫

Andy Pettitte

THROWS: Lefthanded   **MLB CAREER:** 1995–

In a New York Yankees clubhouse boasting such superstars as Derek Jeter and Bernie Williams, and on a pitching staff dominated by such high-profile personalities as Roger Clemens and David Wells, Andy Pettitte quietly has toiled as one of the most effective starting pitchers in the game today. He also was a key figure in the Yankees' string of four World Series titles in five years from 1996–2000. Andy debuted with 12 wins in his rookie season of 1995, then blossomed the following year, when he went

21-8. He hasn't won fewer than 13 games in a season since. Andy doesn't possess a blazing fastball, but the resourceful lefty is a complete pitcher.

BIRTH DATE: June 15, 1972
BORN IN: Baton Rouge, LA
HEIGHT: 6′5″   **WEIGHT:** 225
BATS: Left   **THROWS:** Left

TRIVIA: *In what category does Andy leads the majors since the year of his debut (1995)?*

➤➤➤➤➤➤➤➤➤➤➤➤➤➤➤➤➤➤➤➤➤➤➤➤➤➤➤➤➤➤➤➤➤➤

Mark Prior

THROWS: Righthanded **MLB CAREER:** 2002–

Perhaps not since the Mets' Tom Seaver in the late 1960s had a young pitcher's debut been as eagerly anticipated as Mark Prior's was in 2002. Mark, the second overall pick in the 2001 baseball draft, made only nine minor league starts before the Cubs called him up to the parent club to make his first big-league appearance on May 22. He didn't disappoint, striking out 10 batters and allowing only two runs and four hits in six innings of a 7-4 victory over Pittsburgh. He was in the rotation for good.

Mark went on make 19 starts and finished 6-6 with 147 strikeouts in 116.2 innings. He won 18 games in 2003 with an ERA of 2.43 and 245 strikeouts in 211.1 innings.

BIRTH DATE: September 7, 1980
BORN IN: San Diego, CA
HEIGHT: 6′5″ **WEIGHT:** 225
BATS: Right **THROWS:** Right

TRIVIA: *Who was Mark's first strikeout victim in the Major Leagues?*

Barry Zito

THROWS: Lefthanded **MLB CAREER: 2000–**

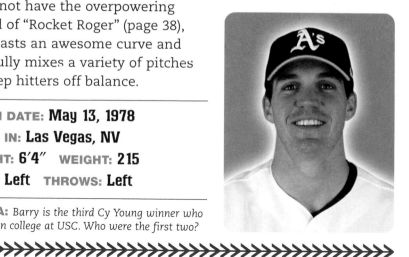

Barry Zito went 11-1 over his final 13 starts for the Oakland A's in 2001, his first full season in the big leagues. But the 23-year-old was just warming up. In 2002, he forged one of the best seasons ever by such a young pitcher. Barry went 23-5 with an ERA of just 2.75, struck out 182 hitters in 229.1 innings, and limited opponents to a meager .218 batting average. At 24, he became the youngest winner of the Cy Young Award since Boston's Roger Clemens, who also was 24, in 1986. While Barry does not have the overpowering speed of "Rocket Roger" (page 38), he boasts an awesome curve and skillfully mixes a variety of pitches to keep hitters off balance.

BIRTH DATE: May 13, 1978
BORN IN: Las Vegas, NV
HEIGHT: 6′4″ **WEIGHT: 215**
BATS: Left **THROWS: Left**

TRIVIA: *Barry is the third Cy Young winner who played in college at USC. Who were the first two?*

>>

Fantastic Fireballers

Few things in sports are more intimidating than a fastball. These players were the fastest.

Kerry Wood led the Majors in strikeouts in 2003; he once struck out 20 batters in one game!

Kevin Brown

THROWS: Righthanded **MLB CAREER: 1986–**

Fiery and competitive Kevin Brown has a well-traveled Major League resumé that includes stints with Texas, Baltimore, Florida, San Diego, and Los Angeles. But wherever he's gone, Kevin has always has been a winner. The Rangers saw that immediately, promoting him to the big club after only six minor league games in 1986. His big breakthrough came in 1992, when he won 21 games for the club. Kevin was the ace of the Marlins' world championship staff in 1997, then helped lead the Padres to the World Series the next year.

Kevin's great fastball is matched by a devastating splitter, but it is his intensity and determination that really sets him apart.

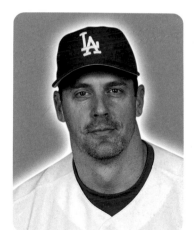

BIRTH DATE: March 14, 1965
BORN IN: Milledgeville, GA
HEIGHT: 6'4" **WEIGHT: 200**
BATS: Right **THROWS: Right**

TRIVIA: *Against what team did Kevin toss his first career no-hitter in 1997?*

>>

Steve Carlton

THROWS: Lefthanded   **MLB CAREER: 1965–1988**

The last-place Philadelphia Phillies won only 59 games in 1972. Remarkably, Steve Carlton won 27 of them. Lefty, as he was called, also led the N.L. by striking out 310 batters that year en route to the first of his four Cy Young Awards. In time, Carlton helped turn the Phillies into winners: In 1980, he won 24 games to help the franchise win its first World Series. Though Lefty had a blistering fastball, he was as cunning as he was overpowering. His real strikeout pitch was a slider, that, in baseball parlance,

"fell off the table." That slider was largely responsible for his 4,136 career strikeouts—the most ever by a lefthander. Steve won 329 games in his Hall of Fame career.

BIRTH DATE: December 22, 1944
BORN IN: Miami, FL
HEIGHT: 6′4″   WEIGHT: 210
BATS: Left   THROWS: Left

TRIVIA: *For what team did Steve notch the first of his six 20-win seasons in 1971?*

>>>

Roger Clemens

THROWS: Righthanded   **MLB CAREER: 1984–2003**

From Boston to Toronto to the New York Yankees, Roger Clemens spent two decades as one of baseball's most feared starting pitchers. "Rocket Roger" sported an explosive fastball that enabled him to become just the third player to fan more than 4,000 batters in his career. Only Nolan Ryan (page 50) and Steve Carlton (page 36) ever struck out more. Roger also shares the big-league record with 20 strikeouts in a game, which he did twice. But he was much more than just a thrower. Roger's

unyielding competitive drive carried him to 310 career victories (he reached the magical 300-win milestone in 2003) and an unprecedented six Cy Young Awards.

BIRTH DATE: August 4, 1962
BORN IN: Dayton, OH
HEIGHT: 6'4"   **WEIGHT: 235**
BATS: Right   **THROWS: Right**

TRIVIA: *How many of his Cy Young Awards did Roger win while with the Blue Jays?*

≫≫≫≫≫≫≫≫≫≫≫≫≫≫≫≫≫≫≫≫≫≫≫≫≫≫

Don Drysdale

THROWS: Righthanded   **MLB CAREER: 1956–1969**

Don Drysdale was the righthanded partner of southpaw Sandy Koufax (page 48), giving the Dodgers the most potent one-two pitching punch in the Major Leagues in the 1960s. Don made his Dodgers debut while the club still was in Brooklyn in 1956, and he won 17 games the following year. He developed into a strikeout pitcher in 1959, when he fanned a league-best 242 batters in 270.2 innings. It was the first of his six 200-plus strikeout seasons in a seven-year span. But as overpowering as

Don was, he also had pinpoint control—which he often used to intimidate batters with a well-timed and well-placed knockdown pitch. Don won 209 games in 14 seasons.

BIRTH DATE: July 23, 1936
BORN IN: Van Nuys, CA
HEIGHT: 6'6"   **WEIGHT: 216**
BATS: Right   **THROWS: Right**

TRIVIA: *Don equaled the N.L. record for home runs by a pitcher in 1965. How many did he hit?*

>>>

Bob Feller

THROWS: Righthanded   **MLB CAREER: 1936–1956**

Today's game boasts flamethrowers such as Randy Johnson and Kerry Wood. Then there are other more recent greats such as Nolan Ryan and Tom Seaver. But talk to almost any old-timer, and they'll tell you that none of them threw a baseball as fast as Bob Feller, a star for Cleveland before and after World War II. "Rapid Robert" was only 17 when he debuted for the Indians in 1936. In his first start, he struck out 15 St. Louis Browns. He went on to win 266 games in 18 seasons, tossed three no-hitters, and led the league in strikeouts seven times. He missed most of four years while in the Navy, but came back in 1946 to win 26 games and fan 348 batters.

BIRTH DATE: November 3, 1918
BORN IN: Van Meter, IA
HEIGHT: 6'0"   WEIGHT: 185
BATS: Right   THROWS: Right

TRIVIA: *Bob shares the MLB record for one-hitters with Nolan Ryan. How many did he have?*

>>

Randy Johnson

THROWS: Lefthanded **MLB CAREER: 1988–**

At 6 feet 10 inches tall and with a steely glare, Randy Johnson strikes one of the most imposing figures ever to take the mound. Add in a 100-miles-per-hour fastball, and you'll find few hitters who relish the chance to dig in at the plate. Randy was a talented, but unpolished, flamethrower who struggled with his control when he debuted with Montreal in 1988. Once he harnessed his wildness, he became dominant. In 1995, he went 18-2 for Seattle and won the A.L. Cy Young Award. Four seasons

later, he signed with Arizona and added the first of four straight N.L. Cy Youngs. He struck out more than 300 batters each of those four years and approached 4,000 for his career.

BIRTH DATE: September 10, 1963
BORN IN: Walnut Creek, CA
HEIGHT: 6'10" **WEIGHT: 230**
BATS: Right **THROWS: Left**

TRIVIA: *Only one player has more Cy Young Awards than Randy, who has five. Who is he?*

>>>

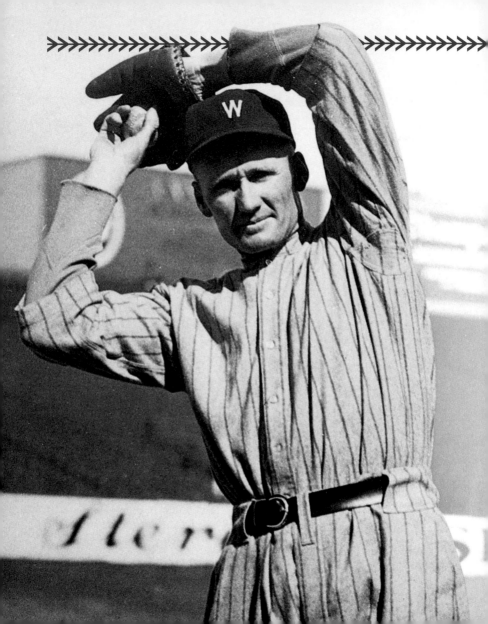

Walter Johnson

THROWS: Righthanded   **MLB CAREER: 1907–1927**

Walter Johnson was the greatest pitcher of his time, and perhaps the greatest of any era. For 10 consecutive seasons from 1910–1919, "Big Train" won at least 20 games. Twice, he won more than 30, topped by 36 in 1913. He led the A.L. in wins six times and in strikeouts 12 times, and finished his career with 417 victories. Only Cy Young, whose career was near its end when Walter's was beginning in 1907, won more games (511). Walter did all this, too, while playing for mostly mediocre Washington Senators teams. They were shut out 65 times when he took the mound. So Walter often took matters into his own hands, shutting out the opponent a record 110 times!

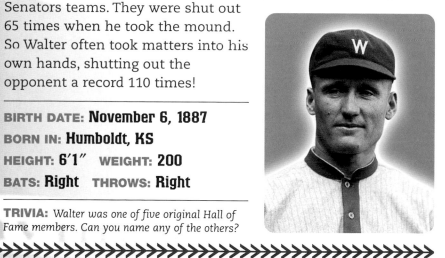

BIRTH DATE: November 6, 1887
BORN IN: Humboldt, KS
HEIGHT: 6'1"   WEIGHT: 200
BATS: Right   THROWS: Right

TRIVIA: *Walter was one of five original Hall of Fame members. Can you name any of the others?*

Sandy Koufax

THROWS: Lefthanded **MLB CAREER: 1955–1966**

Flamethrower Sandy Koufax's career was like a shooting star: It shined very brightly for a brief period then was over in an instant. Sandy struggled with his control early in his big-league career and lost more games than he won from 1955–1960. But he blossomed in 1961, winning 18 games for the Dodgers and leading the league with 269 strikeouts. And for the next several years, he was baseball's best pitcher. He won 25 games in 1963, 26 in 1965, and 27 in 1966. He led the league in strikeouts four times and in ERA five years in a row beginning in 1962. Then, unwilling to risk further injury to a left arm already racked by arthritis, he retired at age 30 following the 1966 season.

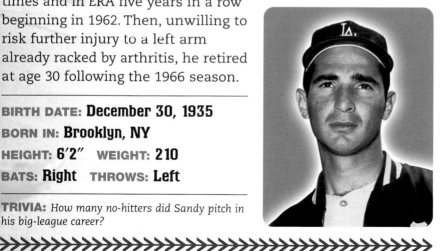

BIRTH DATE: December 30, 1935
BORN IN: Brooklyn, NY
HEIGHT: 6′2″ **WEIGHT: 210**
BATS: Right **THROWS: Left**

TRIVIA: *How many no-hitters did Sandy pitch in his big-league career?*

>>

Nolan Ryan

THROWS: Righthanded   **MLB CAREER: 1966–1993**

Though almost every hitter knew that the "Express" was coming, few ever were able to catch up to it. The Express was Nolan Ryan's fastball, and it topped out at more than 100 miles per hour. Ryan, who pitched for the Mets, Angels, Astros, and Rangers, used his devastating heater to fashion seven no-hitters and strike out 5,714 batters (both are Major League records). He led his league in strikeouts 11 times, the last at age 43 in 1990. Early in his career, Ryan was just a fireballer who struggled with his control and lost as many games as he won. But as he got older, he got wiser—without losing his devastating velocity. He finished his career with 324 wins.

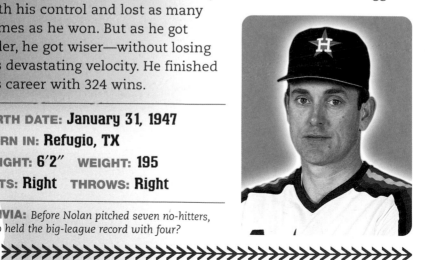

BIRTH DATE: January 31, 1947
BORN IN: Refugio, TX
HEIGHT: 6'2"   **WEIGHT: 195**
BATS: Right   **THROWS: Right**

TRIVIA: *Before Nolan pitched seven no-hitters, who held the big-league record with four?*

>>>

Curt Schilling

THROWS: Righthanded **MLB CAREER: 1988–**

Imagine a pitching staff that features one of the hardest throwers in big-league history. Then add in another fantastic fireballer. What you get are the Arizona Diamondbacks. That club already featured lefthanded flamethrower Randy Johnson before adding righthander Curt Schilling to the mix for the stretch run in 2000. Curt previously had some success in Philadelphia, but he really put it all together in 2001. He went 22-6 with an ERA of 2.98 and 293 strikeouts in 256.2 innings. He finished second to Johnson in the balloting for the Cy Young Award, then helped the Diamondbacks upset the Yankees in a classic World Series. Curt joined the Boston Red Sox for 2004.

BIRTH DATE: November 14, 1966
BORN IN: Anchorage, AK
HEIGHT: 6′5″ **WEIGHT: 205**
BATS: Right **THROWS: Right**

TRIVIA: *With what team did Curt begin his Major League career in 1988?*

>>>

Tom Seaver

THROWS: Righthanded   MLB CAREER: 1967–1986

They called him "Tom Terrific"—and with good reason. From the moment he stepped off the University of Southern California campus and into the New York Mets organization in 1967 as one of the most talked-about young players of his time, Tom was terrific. He won 311 games in 20 big-league seasons, most of them with the Mets and Cincinnati Reds, and earned 12 All-Star selections. He struck out 3,640 batters, including at least 200 in a record nine consecutive seasons from 1968–1976. More

importantly, he helped turn the Mets, lovable losers since joining the N.L. in 1962, into winners. He won 25 games in 1969, the year the "Miracle Mets" won their first world title.

BIRTH DATE: November 17, 1944
BORN IN: Fresno, CA
HEIGHT: 6'1"   WEIGHT: 206
BATS: Right   THROWS: Right

TRIVIA: *What is the name of the New York Mets home ballpark?*

>>

Kerry Wood

THROWS: Righthanded   **MLB CAREER: 1998–**

Kerry Wood announced his presence on the Major League scene in a big way in 1998. The 20-year-old was making only his fifth career start when he struck out a record-tying 20 Houston Astros in a 2-0 victory at Wrigley Field on May 6. Kerry's blazing fastball, combined with a wicked roundhouse curve, helped him strike out 233 batters in just 166.2 innings in 1998. He also won 13 of 19 decisions en route to earning N.L Rookie of the Year honors. Though he missed all of the 1999 season due to reconstructive elbow surgery, Kerry returned to fan 132 batters in 137 innings in 2000, then began a string of three consecutive 200-plus strikeout seasons the next year.

BIRTH DATE: June 16, 1977
BORN IN: Irving, TX
HEIGHT: 6′5″   WEIGHT: 230
BATS: Right   THROWS: Right

TRIVIA: *In addition to Kerry, who are the only other pitchers to strike out 20 batters in a game?*

Hurling Heroes

WHETHER IN THE HALL
OF FAME OR ON THE WAY,
THESE PITCHERS ARE
AMONG HISTORY'S
GREATEST MOUNDSMEN.

*Catfish Hunter helped both the
Oakland A's and the New York
Yankees to World Series wins.*

Grover Alexander

THROWS: Righthanded   **MLB CAREER: 1911–1930**

Grover Cleveland Alexander was a workhorse who started 599 games in his 20-year big-league career. More often than not, he completed what he started, and logged more than 300 innings nine times with the Phillies and Cubs. But it was one of his shortest stints that made him a hero to St. Louis Cardinals fans. It came in Game 7 of the 1926 World Series against the Yankees. He already had won two games, including Game 6, with complete-game stints when he came on in relief in the seventh inning with the bases loaded and St. Louis clinging to a 3-2 lead. He struck out Tony Lazzeri to end the threat, then closed out the Yankees the rest of the way to save the win.

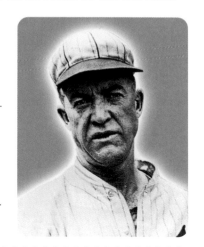

BIRTH DATE: February 26, 1887
BORN IN: Elba, NE
HEIGHT: 6′1″   WEIGHT: 185
BATS: Right   THROWS: Right

TRIVIA: *Grover Cleveland won 373 career games. How many N.L. hurlers ever won more?*

Dizzy Dean

THROWS: Righthanded   **MLB CAREER: 1930–1947**

Dizzy Dean's antics on and off the field had already made him a popular figure with St. Louis Cardinals fans and his "Gashouse Gang" teammates in the early 1930s. Then, his masterful pitching performance in Game 7 of the 1934 World Series earned him a permanent place in that city's baseball lore. After going 30-7 during the regular season and leading the league in strikeouts for the third of four consecutive seasons, Dizzy (his given name was Jay) won Game 1 of the World Series against Detroit. Later, with the Series tied at three games each, he pitched the finale on one day's rest. Dizzy blanked the Tigers 11-0 on six hits to give the Cardinals the world title.

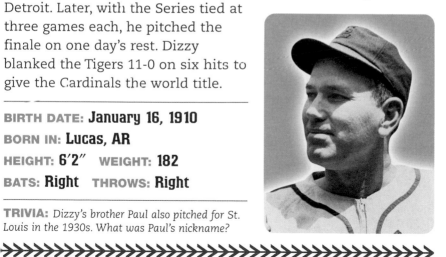

BIRTH DATE: January 16, 1910
BORN IN: Lucas, AR
HEIGHT: 6′2″   WEIGHT: 182
BATS: Right   THROWS: Right

TRIVIA: *Dizzy's brother Paul also pitched for St. Louis in the 1930s. What was Paul's nickname?*

>>

Lefty Grove

THROWS: Lefthanded   **MLB CAREER: 1925–1941**

Lefty Grove never wanted to be photographed with a baseball in his throwing hand for fear that an opposing hitter might pick up on something that would help him at the plate. He needn't have worried. Lefty won 300 games and lost only 141 in his 17-year career with the Philadelphia Athletics and Boston Braves. He led the league in wins four times, in strikeouts seven times, and in ERA nine times. More importantly, he helped pitch the Athletics to three consecutive A.L. pennants from 1929–1931.

Lefty was a combined 79-15 in those years with 68 complete games in his 99 starts and an ERA of just 2.46. The Athletics went on to win the World Series in 1929 and 1930.

BIRTH DATE: March 6, 1900
BORN IN: Lonaconing, MD
HEIGHT: 6'3"   WEIGHT: 190
BATS: Left   THROWS: Left

TRIVIA: *Grove almost always was called Lefty. What was his given name?*

>>

Catfish Hunter

THROWS: Righthanded **MLB CAREER: 1965–1979**

Catfish Hunter was the ace of the pitching staff that helped the Oakland A's become a dynasty in the early 1970s. From 1971–1974, Catfish won more than 20 games each year, and each year Oakland won the A.L. West. In 1974, he won a career-best 25 games and helped lead the A's to their third consecutive World Series triumph. Catfish also became one of the first big-name free agents when a judge ruled that the A's had broken his contract that year. He signed with the Yankees for $3.5 million— a huge amount at the time—and won 23 games in 1975, his first season with his new club. Then he helped New York win three consecutive pennants, 1976–1978.

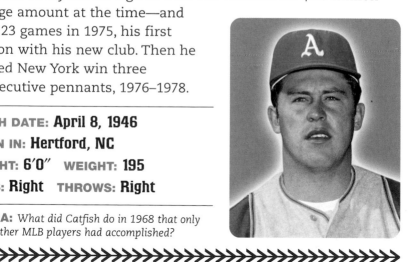

BIRTH DATE: April 8, 1946
BORN IN: Hertford, NC
HEIGHT: 6'0" **WEIGHT: 195**
BATS: Right **THROWS: Right**

TRIVIA: *What did Catfish do in 1968 that only eight other MLB players had accomplished?*

>>>

Greg Maddux

THROWS: Righthanded   **MLB CAREER: 1986–**

Greg Maddux doesn't really look the part. He doesn't have the scowl of Roger Clemens, the physique of Curt Schilling, or the fastball of Randy Johnson. He looks more like an accountant at a company softball game than one of the greatest big-league pitchers of our time. But, in fact, no pitcher in history, not even legendary Cy Young, was as consistent a winner as Greg has been. For a record 16 consecutive seasons starting in 1988 while he was with the Cubs, Greg won at least 15 games (he broke Young's mark of 15 years in a row).

In 1992, his last season in Chicago, Greg won the Cy Young Award. Then he signed with the Braves in 1993 and won it three more times.

BIRTH DATE: April 14, 1966
BORN IN: San Angelo, TX
HEIGHT: 6'0"   **WEIGHT: 185**
BATS: Right   **THROWS: Right**

TRIVIA: *Besides Greg, who is the only other pitcher to win four straight Cy Young Awards?*

Juan Marichal

THROWS: Righthanded **MLB CAREER: 1960–1975**

The Giants knew they had a special pitcher the first time Juan Marichal took the mound: He shut out the Phillies on one hit in his debut in 1960. Marichal was a hero to San Francisco fans who watched him compile six 20-win seasons in a seven-year span from 1963–1969. But he was also a hero to a generation of Latin American players and fans. Marichal's 243 career victories stood as the most by a Latin American pitcher until Dennis Martinez (page 14) eclipsed the mark. Today, Major League rosters are filled with players from Latin America. But it was early stars such as Marichal, Roberto Clemente, and the Alou brothers (Felipe, Jesus, and Matty) who helped pave the way.

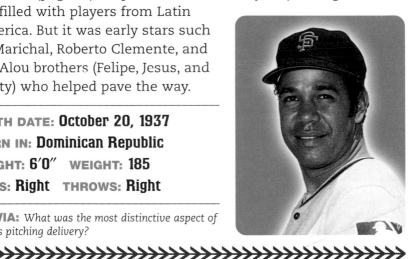

BIRTH DATE: October 20, 1937
BORN IN: Dominican Republic
HEIGHT: 6'0" **WEIGHT: 185**
BATS: Right **THROWS: Right**

TRIVIA: *What was the most distinctive aspect of Juan's pitching delivery?*

>>>

Don Newcombe

THROWS: Righthanded **MLB CAREER: 1949–1960**

Jackie Robinson shattered baseball's color barrier with Brooklyn in 1947. Two years later, Robinson was joined on the Dodgers roster by Don Newcombe, who became the first star pitcher who was African-American. Don was an immediate success in Brooklyn, winning 17 games as a rookie in 1949 and helping the Dodgers win the N.L. pennant. That same year, he joined teammates Robinson and Roy Campanella, plus the Cleveland Indians' Larry Doby, as the first African-Americans to play in baseball's annual All-Star Game.

"Newk" went on to win 149 games in 10 seasons. His best year came in 1956, when he was 27-7 for the pennant-winning Dodgers.

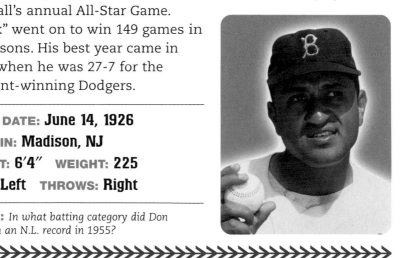

BIRTH DATE: June 14, 1926
BORN IN: Madison, NJ
HEIGHT: 6′4″ **WEIGHT: 225**
BATS: Left **THROWS: Right**

TRIVIA: *In what batting category did Don establish an N.L. record in 1955?*

>>>

Satchel Paige

THROWS: Righthanded   **MLB CAREER: 1948–1953, 1965**

Satchel Paige may have been the best pitcher of his time. However, he didn't make it to the Majors until late in his career, after Major League Baseball's color barrier was broken in 1947. Paige was a star in the Negro Leagues, once going 31-4 for the Pittsburgh Crawfords and helping the Kansas City Monarchs win five pennants. He finally made it to the majors at age 42 in 1948, one year after Jackie Robinson's debut with the Dodgers. He helped the Indians capture the A.L. pennant that year by winning six of seven decisions, but was just 28-31 in five years in the majors. In 1965, at age 59, he pitched three scoreless innings in a game for the Kansas City A's.

BIRTH DATE: July 7, 1906
BORN IN: Mobile, AL
HEIGHT: 6′3″   WEIGHT: 180
BATS: Right THROWS: Right

TRIVIA: *What was the most famous of Satchel's "Rules to Live By"?*

Warren Spahn

THROWS: Lefthanded   **MLB CAREER: 1942–1965**

In 1948, the Boston Braves cruised to the N.L. pennant by pinning their hopes on "Spahn and Sain and two days of rain." Johnny Sain was the real star that year, winning a league-best 24 games, but in time Warren Spahn became the ace of the Braves' staff, first in Boston and then in Milwaukee. Warren won 20 or more games 13 times in a 17-season span from 1947–1963. He led the league in wins eight times, in strikeouts and innings pitched four times, and in ERA three times. Warren was a workhorse who pitched until he was 44 years old and retired with more wins (363) than any other lefthander in big-league history. He tossed no-hitters at age 39 and 40.

BIRTH DATE: April 23, 1921
BORN IN: Buffalo, NY
HEIGHT: 6′0″   **WEIGHT: 175**
BATS: Left   **THROWS: Left**

TRIVIA: *In what batting category did Warren establish an N.L. career record?*

Hoyt Wilhelm

THROWS: Righthanded   **MLB CAREER: 1952–1972**

Hoyt Wilhelm was an ageless wonder who was still pitching to big-league hitters at age 49 in 1972. Wilhelm was a master of the knuckleball, a pitch that is easy on the arm and was the key to his longevity. He didn't make his big-league debut until he was 28 in 1952, when he went 15-3 for the New York Giants while appearing in 71 games, the most in the league. Over the next two decades, he appeared in 999 more games, almost all of them in relief, for various clubs. But he also tossed a no-hitter for Baltimore in 1958 and won 15 games in 1959, his lone season as a full-time starter. Hoyt retired holding all-time records for games pitched (1,070) and wins in relief (124).

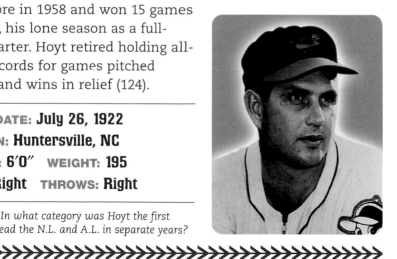

BIRTH DATE: July 26, 1922
BORN IN: Huntersville, NC
HEIGHT: 6'0"   WEIGHT: 195
BATS: Right   THROWS: Right

TRIVIA: *In what category was Hoyt the first player to lead the N.L. and A.L. in separate years?*

>>>>>>>>>>>>>>>>>>>>>>>>>>>>>>>>>>>>>>>

Smokey Joe Wood

THROWS: Righthanded   **MLB CAREER: 1908–1922**

"There's no man alive who can throw harder than Smokey Joe Wood," said Walter Johnson, himself one of the hardest throwers of his or any era. Smokey Joe won a relatively modest 116 games in his big-league career. But in 1912, he fashioned one of the most remarkable years any hurler ever had. Smokey Joe made 38 starts for the Boston Red Sox that year. He completed 35 of them, 10 by shutout, and went 34-5 with an ERA of 1.91. Then he went on to win three games in the World Series, including the finale, as the Red Sox edged the New York Giants. An injury ended Smokey Joe's pitching career prematurely, though he continued to play in the outfield.

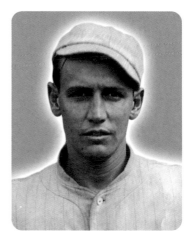

BIRTH DATE: October 25, 1889
BORN IN: Kansas City, MO
HEIGHT: 5′11″   WEIGHT: 180
BATS: Right   THROWS: Right

TRIVIA: *What Giants future Hall of Fame great did Smokey Joe beat in the 1912 Series finale?*

>>

Cy Young

THROWS: Righthanded **MLB CAREER: 1890–1911**

Just looking at Denton True "Cy" Young's statistics might be enough to give any of today's pitchers a sore arm. And yet, despite hurling 7,300-plus innings in 22 seasons, Cy never had an arm problem. He broke into the majors in 1890 with the N.L.'s Cleveland Spiders, then won 27 games his first full season with the club in 1891. Cy went on to win 30 or more games five times, including 36 in 1892, and 511 in his career—far and away the big-league record. He almost always completed his starts (749 of 815

in his career), and once pitched 453 innings in a season. In 1956, one year after his death, MLB began issuing the Cy Young Award annually to the game's best pitcher.

BIRTH DATE: March 29, 1867
BORN IN: Gilmore, OH
HEIGHT: 6'2" **WEIGHT: 210**
BATS: Right **THROWS: Right**

TRIVIA: *What does the "Cy" in Cy Young's name stand for?*

>>>

Series Stars

IN THE PRESSURE COOKER THAT IS THE WORLD SERIES, THESE PITCHERS CAME THROUGH WITH THE BIGGEST WINS.

Jack Morris was a World Series pitching star for the Tigers in 1984 and the Twins in 1991.

Lew Burdette

THROWS: Righthanded **MLB CAREER: 1950–1967**

Lew Burdette won 17 games for the Milwaukee Braves during the 1957 regular season. But that hardly prepared the mighty New York Yankees for what was to come in the World Series that year, when Lew turned in one of the most masterful pitching performances in history. The Yankees entered the Series with six titles since 1949, and they won Game 1. But Lew evened the Series with a 4-2 win in Game 2, and later won Game 5 1-0 to put the Braves ahead three games to two. After the Yankees forced a decisive seventh game, Lew came back on two days' rest. He shut out the Yankees again 5-0, running his scoreless streak to 24 innings and giving the Braves the title.

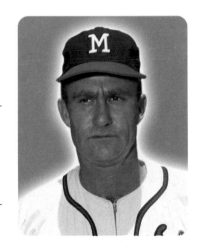

BIRTH DATE: November 22, 1926
BORN IN: Nitro, WV
HEIGHT: 6′2″ **WEIGHT: 190**
BATS: Right **THROWS: Right**

TRIVIA: *What team beat Lew in Game 7 of the World Series in 1958?*

>>

Whitey Ford

THROWS: Lefthanded   **MLB CAREER: 1950–1967**

Bronx Bombers such as Mickey Mantle, Roger Maris, and others helped carry the powerful New York Yankees to World Series after World Series in the 1950s and 1960s. And once they got there, the Yankees turned over the ball to reliable Whitey Ford. Whitey won more games in the World Series (10) while pitching more innings (146) and striking out more batters (94) than any other pitcher in history. He was on the mound for so many key moments in the Yankees' World Series history that his regular-season accomplishments often are taken for granted. But he won 236 career games, including 25 in 1961, when he earned the Cy Young Award.

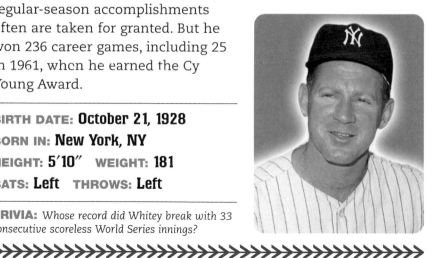

BIRTH DATE: October 21, 1928
BORN IN: New York, NY
HEIGHT: 5′10″   WEIGHT: 181
BATS: Left   THROWS: Left

TRIVIA: *Whose record did Whitey break with 33 consecutive scoreless World Series innings?*

>>>

Bob Gibson

THROWS: Righthanded   **MLB CAREER: 1959–1975**

Only two months after breaking his leg during a regular-season game, Bob Gibson came back to deliver a masterful performance in the 1967 World Series. The fireballing Gibson, famous for protecting the plate by pitching inside, won three games for the Cardinals against the Red Sox in that season's Fall Classic. He went the distance in Games 1, 4, and 7, winning the finale 7-2. Bob's fantastic World Series was a prelude to an unbelievable season the next year. He won 22 games in 1968 while posting an ERA of 1.12, the lowest in 54 years. He led the league with 13 shutouts and 268 strikeouts, while opposing hitters batted a feeble .184 against him.

BIRTH DATE: November 9, 1935
BORN IN: Omaha, NE
HEIGHT: 6′1″   **WEIGHT: 195**
BATS: Right   **THROWS: Right**

TRIVIA: *In what sport did Bob, an all-around great athlete, earn a college scholarship?*

⟫⟫⟫⟫⟫⟫⟫⟫⟫⟫⟫⟫⟫⟫⟫⟫⟫⟫⟫⟫⟫⟫⟫⟫⟫⟫⟫⟫⟫⟫⟫⟫⟫

Orel Hershiser

THROWS: Righthanded   **MLB CAREER: 1983–2000**

Former Dodgers manager Tommy Lasorda called Orel Hershiser the "Bulldog." That nickname was never more deserved than late in the 1988 regular season and into the postseason, when the gritty Hershiser helped carry Los Angeles to the world championship. Orel, who won 23 of 31 decisions that year, finished the season with a Major League record 59 consecutive scoreless innings. Then he started three games and saved one in a seven-game League Championship Series against the Mets. In the World Series against the A's, Orel won two games and was the MVP. He finished his career with more than 200 victories (204) and 2,000 strikeouts (2,014).

BIRTH DATE: September 16, 1958
BORN IN: Buffalo, NY
HEIGHT: 6'3"   WEIGHT: 192
BATS: Right   THROWS: Right

TRIVIA: *In addition to the Dodgers, for what club did Orel pitch in the World Series?*

Don Larsen

THROWS: Righthanded   **MLB CAREER: 1953–1967**

Don Larsen was a journeyman pitcher who won only 81 career games in 14 big-league seasons for eight different franchises. But for one afternoon in 1956, he was perfect…literally. On October 8, 1956, Don pitched the only perfect game in World Series history, beating Brooklyn 2-0. Twenty-seven Dodgers' hitters came to the plate, and 27 hitters went down. No Brooklyn player reached base. Don struck out seven, and needed only 97 pitches to complete his gem. Don's masterpiece not only earned

him his place in baseball lore, it also was a pivotal point in the Series. The win put the Yankees ahead three games to two, and they went on to win the title in seven games.

BIRTH DATE: August 7, 1929
BORN IN: Michigan City, IN
HEIGHT: 6′4″   WEIGHT: 227
BATS: Right   THROWS: Right

TRIVIA: *What Hall of Fame player was the Yankees' catcher during Don's perfect game?*

≫≫≫≫≫≫≫≫≫≫≫≫≫≫≫≫≫≫≫≫≫≫≫≫≫≫≫≫≫≫≫≫≫≫≫≫≫

Christy Mathewson

THROWS: Righthanded   **MLB CAREER: 1900–1916**

Christy Mathewson won 373 career games. He posted more 20-win seasons (12) than any other hurler in N.L. history. And he was one of the original electees to the Baseball Hall of Fame in 1936. But it was his performance in the 1905 World Series, when he led the Giants over Philadelphia by tossing three shutouts in a six-day span, that made him a legend. It started in Game 1, when he blanked the Athletics on four hits. After Philadelphia tied the Series with a win in Game 2, Christy came back on two days' rest to win Game 3 9-0. Two days later, he ended the Series with a 2-0 shutout. The final tally: 27 innings, no runs, only 14 hits allowed, and 18 strikeouts with just one walk.

BIRTH DATE: August 12, 1880
BORN IN: Factoryville, PA
HEIGHT: 6′1″   **WEIGHT: 195**
BATS: Right   **THROWS: Right**

TRIVIA: *One of Christy's nicknames was, naturally, "Matty." What was the other?*

>>>

Jack Morris

THROWS: Righthanded   **MLB CAREER: 1977–1994**

Jack Morris won 254 regular-season games in his big-league career. He was a five-time All-Star, pitched for world-championship teams in Detroit, Minnesota, and Toronto, and struck out 2,478 batters while compiling a lifetime ERA of 3.90. But Jack's 18 big-league seasons are best summed up by his masterful pitching performance in Game 7 of the 1991 World Series. Jack was already considered one of the game's best clutch pitchers, but he cemented that reputation with a 10-inning, seven-hit shutout of the Atlanta Braves while pitching for his hometown Twins that year. Minnesota won the final game 1-0, and Jack was named the Series MVP.

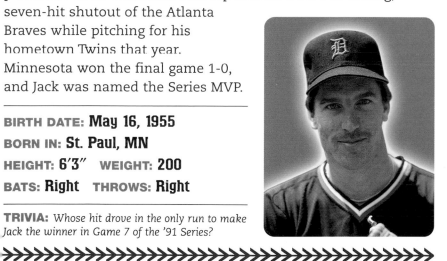

BIRTH DATE: May 16, 1955
BORN IN: St. Paul, MN
HEIGHT: 6'3"   **WEIGHT: 200**
BATS: Right   **THROWS: Right**

TRIVIA: *Whose hit drove in the only run to make Jack the winner in Game 7 of the '91 Series?*

⫸⫸⫸⫸⫸⫸⫸⫸⫸⫸⫸⫸⫸⫸⫸⫸⫸⫸⫸⫸⫸⫸⫸⫸

Clutch Closers

WITH THE GAME ON THE LINE, THESE ARE THE PITCHERS MANAGERS CALL ON TO SHUT DOWN THE OPPOSING TEAM.

As great as Mariano Rivera has been in the regular season, he's even better in the postseason.

Dennis Eckersley

THROWS: Righthanded   **MLB CAREER: 1975–1998**

For the first half of his 24-year big-league career, Dennis Eckersley was an effective starting pitcher who won 151 games, topped by 20 wins for Boston in 1978. But shortly before the 1987 season opener, Dennis was traded from Chicago to Oakland, where his career underwent an amazing transformation. The A's moved Dennis to the bullpen, and he developed into one of baseball's elite closers over the next decade. Dennis combined his effective slider with unbelievable

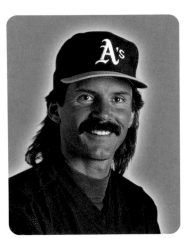

control (in 1990, for instance, he struck out 73 batters while walking only four in 73.1 innings) to save 386 games for Oakland and St. Louis from 1987–1997.

BIRTH DATE: October 3, 1954
BORN IN: Oakland, CA
HEIGHT: 6′2″   WEIGHT: 190
BATS: Right   THROWS: Right

TRIVIA: *How many times was Dennis named to the A.L.'s All-Star team?*

>>

Rollie Fingers

THROWS: Righthanded   **MLB CAREER: 1968–1985**

With his trademark handlebar mustache, Rollie Fingers looked like a player from long ago. Instead, he was the premier closer of his time. A former starting pitcher who was banished to the bullpen early in his big-league career, Rollie helped the Oakland A's win three consecutive world titles from 1972–1974 by making 201 relief appearances, saving 59 games, and fashioning an ERA of 2.34 in that span. He led his league in saves three times, including 1981, when he had 28 for Milwaukee

and was named the A.L.'s MVP and Cy Young Award winner. When he retired in 1985, Rollie was tops on baseball's all-time list with 341 career saves.

BIRTH DATE: August 25, 1946
BORN IN: Steubenville, OH
HEIGHT: 6'4"   WEIGHT: 195
BATS: Right   THROWS: Right

TRIVIA: *True or false: Rollie grew his famous mustache when the A's owner paid him to.*

>>

Eric Gagné

THROWS: Righthanded   **MLB CAREER: 1999–**

With his scraggly goatee, rumpled uniform, and menacing glare, Eric Gagné is a throwback to intimidating closers such as Goose Gossage and Al Hrabosky. Just as intimidating, though, is a fastball that nears 100 miles per hour and a devastating curve that leaves batters frozen helplessly at the plate. Gagné originally was one of the Dodgers' top starting prospects, but Los Angeles, desperate for a closer in 2002, moved him to the bullpen that year. He responded with a club-record 52 saves, then was nearly unhittable in 2003. That year, he saved 55 games, struck out 137 batters in 82.1 innings, and was named the N.L.'s Cy Young Award winner.

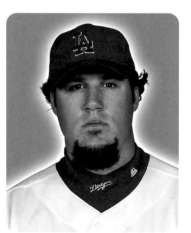

BIRTH DATE: January 7, 1976
BORN IN: Montreal, Quebec, Canada
HEIGHT: 6′2″   WEIGHT: 195
BATS: Right   THROWS: Right

TRIVIA: *Eric set the record for successful saves in a row. How many did he have (through 2003)?*

>>>

Troy Percival

THROWS: **Righthanded**   **MLB CAREER:** **1995–**

The Angels thought so highly of Troy Percival that in 1996, they traded Lee Smith, baseball's all-time saves leader, and handed the closer's job to Troy. He rewarded his club's faith by saving 36 games that year, and he's been the Angels' steady closer ever since. Troy averaged 35 saves from 1996–2003, including a career-best 42 in 1998. He had 40 saves during the 2002 regular season, then closed out three games against the San Francisco Giants in the World Series, including the Angels' decisive Game 7 triumph. Troy possesses a blistering fastball that has enabled him to average well over one strikeout per inning over the course of his career.

BIRTH DATE: **August 9, 1969**
BORN IN: **Fontana, CA**
HEIGHT: **6'3"**   **WEIGHT:** **200**
BATS: **Right**   **THROWS:** **Right**

TRIVIA: *Of Anaheim's 11 postseason wins in 2002, how many did Troy save?*

>>

Mariano Rivera

THROWS: Righthanded   **MLB CAREER:** 1995–

A closer learns to operate every day in pressure situations. And the pressure is never more intense than in the postseason, when every pitch is scrutinized by hordes of media and millions of fans watching on television. Mariano Rivera has thrived on just such a stage, however, to become the most dominant postseason closer in history. Mariano took over as the Yankees' closer in 1997 and averaged nearly 40 saves per season through 2003. And in the postseason, he has been just about unhittable. Through 2002, he was 6-1 with 25 saves and an ERA of 0.79 in postseason play. He closed out Yankees World Series titles in 1998, 1999, and 2000.

BIRTH DATE: November 29, 1969
BORN IN: Panama City, Panama
HEIGHT: 6′2″   **WEIGHT:** 170
BATS: Right   **THROWS:** Right

TRIVIA: *Through 2003, Mariano was first on the Yankees' career saves list. Who was second?*

>>

Lee Smith

THROWS: Righthanded   **MLB CAREER: 1980–1997**

Lee Smith stood 6 feet 6 inches and weighed 225 pounds during his playing career. And on each pitch he hurtled that hulking frame toward the batter with everything he had. Lee rarely tried to fool batters, and yet hitters rarely could solve the man who is baseball's all-time saves leader. A fierce competitor, Smith saved 478 games in his 18-year big-league career with eight clubs. He led his league in saves four times, and became only the second player to record 30 or more saves in four consecutive seasons while with the Cubs from 1984–1987. But his best years came with St. Louis, for whom he saved 160 games in a four-year span from 1990–1993.

BIRTH DATE: December 4, 1957
BORN IN: Shreveport, LA
HEIGHT: 6'6"   **WEIGHT: 225**
BATS: Right   **THROWS: Right**

TRIVIA: *Whom did Lee succeed as baseball's all-time saves leader?*

>>>

John Smoltz

THROWS: Righthanded   **MLB CAREER: 1988–**

Just like Dennis Eckersley did in the 1980s, John Smoltz moved from the starting rotation to the bullpen to become one of baseball's premier closers in the early 2000s. Not even Eck, though, had as much success as John had before switching roles. He won 157 games in 12 seasons as a starter from 1988–1999, including 24 in 1996, when he won the N.L. Cy Young Award. After John missed all of the 2000 season to injury, he shifted to closer late in 2001. The move suited him well. In 2002, his first full season in his new role, John saved 55 games and was baseball's Fireman of the Year. He had 45 more saves before tendinitis sidelined him in August, 2003.

BIRTH DATE: May 15, 1967
BORN IN: Detroit, MI
HEIGHT: 6'3"   WEIGHT: 210
BATS: Right   THROWS: Right

TRIVIA: *John's 55 saves in 2002 set an N.L. record. What players shared the mark before him?*

Statistics

THIS SECTION CONTAINS
COMPLETE CAREER
STATISTICS FOR ALL FIFTY
PLAYERS IN THIS BOOK
(UPDATED THROUGH 2003).

Randy Johnson's fastball has
helped him lead his league in
strikeouts eight times.

Grover Alexander
(for more information, see pages 60–61)

Year	Team	W	L	G	GS	CG	SV	IP	BB	SO	ERA
1911	Philadelphia	**28**	13	48	37	**31**	3	**367.0**	129	227	2.57
1912	Philadelphia	19	17	46	34	25	3	**310.1**	105	**195**	2.81
1913	Philadelphia	22	8	47	36	23	2	306.1	75	159	2.79
1914	Philadelphia	**27**	15	46	39	**32**	1	**355.0**	76	**214**	2.38
1915	Philadelphia	**31**	10	49	42	**36**	3	**376.1**	64	**241**	**1.22**
1916	Philadelphia	**33**	12	48	**45**	**38**	3	**389.0**	50	167	**1.55**
1917	Philadelphia	**30**	13	45	**44**	**34**	0	**388.0**	56	**200**	1.83
1918	Chicago Cubs	2	1	3	3	3	0	26.0	3	15	1.73
1919	Chicago Cubs	16	11	30	27	20	1	235.0	38	121	**1.72**
1920	Chicago Cubs	**27**	14	46	**40**	**33**	5	**363.1**	69	**173**	**1.91**
1921	Chicago Cubs	15	13	31	30	21	1	252.0	33	77	3.39
1922	Chicago Cubs	16	13	33	31	20	1	245.2	34	48	3.63
1923	Chicago Cubs	22	12	39	36	26	2	305.0	30	72	3.19
1924	Chicago Cubs	12	5	21	20	12	0	169.1	25	33	3.03
1925	Chicago Cubs	15	11	32	30	20	0	236.0	29	63	3.39
1926	Chicago Cubs	3	3	7	7	4	0	52.0	7	12	3.46
1926	St. Louis	9	7	23	16	11	2	148.1	24	35	2.91
1927	St. Louis	21	10	37	30	22	3	268.0	38	48	2.52
1928	St. Louis	16	9	34	31	18	2	243.2	37	59	3.36
1929	St. Louis	9	8	22	19	8	0	132.0	23	33	3.89
1930	Philadelphia	0	3	9	3	0	0	21.2	6	6	9.14
Totals		**373**	**208**	**696**	**599**	**437**	**32**	**5190.0**	**951**	**2198**	**2.56**

Bold = Led league

Notes
>Elected to the Hall of Fame in 1938;
>Appeared in three World Series (1915, 1926, and 1928) and posted a 3-2 record and a 3.56 ERA;
>Won pitching's unofficial Triple Crown (leading the league in wins, ERA, and strikeouts) in 1915, 1916, and 1920;
>Set a modern rookie record with 28 victories in 1911;
>Hurled record for shutouts in a season (16 in 1916);
>N.L. all-time record holder in victories (373) and shutouts (90);
>His 1.22 ERA in 1915 is the tenth-best single-season ERA of the post-1900 era;
>Served in military during World War I, which is why he missed most of 1918, and wound up deaf in one ear from his experience in France during the war.

Kevin Brown (for more information, see pages 34–35)

Year	Team	W	L	G	GS	CG	SV	IP	BB	SO	ERA
1986	Texas	1	0	1	1	0	0	5.0	0	4	3.60
1988	Texas	1	1	4	4	1	0	23.1	8	12	4.24
1989	Texas	12	9	28	28	7	0	191.0	70	104	3.35
1990	Texas	12	10	26	26	6	0	180.0	60	88	3.60
1991	Texas	9	12	33	33	0	0	210.2	90	96	4.40
1992	Texas	**21**	11	35	35	11	0	**265.2**	76	173	3.32
1993	Texas	15	12	34	34	12	0	233.0	74	142	3.59
1994	Texas	7	9	26	**25**	3	0	170.0	50	123	4.82
1995	Baltimore	10	9	26	26	3	0	172.1	48	117	3.60
1996	Florida	17	11	32	32	5	0	233.0	33	159	**1.89**
1997	Florida	16	8	33	33	6	0	237.1	66	205	2.69
1998	San Diego	18	7	36	**35**	7	0	257.0	49	257	2.38
1999	Los Angeles	18	9	35	**35**	5	0	252.1	59	221	3.00
2000	Los Angeles	13	6	33	33	5	0	230.0	47	216	**2.58**
2001	Los Angeles	10	4	20	19	1	0	115.2	38	104	2.65
2002	Los Angeles	3	4	17	10	0	0	63.2	23	58	4.81
2003	Los Angeles	14	9	32	32	0	0	211.0	56	185	2.39
Totals		**197**	**131**	**451**	**441**	**72**	**0**	**3051.0**	**847**	**2264**	**3.16**

Bold = Led league

Notes

>Six-time All-Star (1992, 1996–1998, 2000, and 2003);
>In 1992, he became the first Texas pitcher to start an All-Star game;
>Twice finished in the top three in voting for the Cy Young Award (second in 1996 and third in 1998);
>Appeared in six postseason series and two World Series (1997 and 1998);
>Hurled no-hitter for Florida against San Francisco in 1997—the only baserunner reached when Kevin hit Marvin Benard with a pitch in the eighth inning;
>Set a postseason record with 46 strikeouts (in 39.1 innings) in 1998;
>His 16 strikeouts for San Diego against Houston in Game 1 of the 1998 Division Series were the second-most ever in a postseason game;
>After only six minor-league appearances (just two starts), he started and defeated Oakland in his first Major League game in 1986;
>One of three pitchers (Jim Abbott, Bobby Witt) in the 1980s to earn his first professional victory in the majors.

Lew Burdette (for more information, see pages 86–87)

Year	Team	W	L	G	GS	CG	SV	IP	BB	SO	ERA
1950	N.Y. Yankees	0	0	2	0	0	0	1.1	0	0	6.75
1951	Boston Braves	0	0	3	0	0	0	4.1	5	1	6.23
1952	Boston Braves	6	11	45	9	5	7	137.0	47	47	3.61
1953	Mil. Braves	15	5	46	13	6	8	175.0	56	58	3.24
1954	Mil. Braves	15	14	38	32	13	0	238.0	62	79	2.76
1955	Mil. Braves	13	8	42	33	11	0	230.0	73	70	4.03
1956	Mil. Braves	19	10	39	35	16	1	256.1	52	110	**2.70**
1957	Mil. Braves	17	9	37	33	14	0	256.2	59	78	3.72
1958	Mil. Braves	20	10	40	36	19	0	275.1	50	113	2.91
1959	Mil. Braves	**21**	15	41	**39**	20	1	289.2	38	105	4.07
1960	Mil. Braves	19	13	45	32	**18**	4	275.2	35	83	3.36
1961	Mil. Braves	18	11	40	36	14	0	**272.1**	33	92	4.00
1962	Mil. Braves	10	9	37	19	6	2	143.2	23	59	4.89
1963	Mil. Braves	6	5	15	13	4	0	84.0	24	28	3.64
1963	St. Louis	3	8	21	14	3	2	98.0	16	45	3.77
1964	St. Louis	1	0	8	0	0	0	10.0	3	3	1.80
1964	Chicago Cubs	9	9	28	17	8	0	131.0	19	40	4.88
1965	Chicago Cubs	0	2	7	3	0	0	20.1	4	5	5.31
1965	Philadelphia	3	3	19	9	1	0	70.2	17	23	5.48
1966	California	7	2	54	0	0	5	79.2	12	27	3.39
1967	California	1	0	19	0	0	1	18.1	0	8	4.91
Totals		**203**	**144**	**626**	**373**	**158**	**31**	**3067.1**	**628**	**1074**	**3.66**

Bold = Led league

Notes
> Two-time All-Star (1957, 1959);
> Appeared in two World Series (1957–1958) and posted a 4-2 record with a 2.92 ERA, highlighted by his MVP performance in 1957;
> Finished third in the 1958 Cy Young Award voting;
> Hurled a no-hitter against Philadelphia at County Stadium on August 18, 1960;
> Ranked in the top three in innings pitched five consecutive seasons (1957–1961);
> Twice led the N.L. in shutouts (with six in 1956 and four in 1959);
> In 1951, he was traded along with $50,000 from the Yankees to the Braves for pitcher Johnny Sain, who won 35 more games in his career before retiring in 1955—Burdette won 155 games for the Braves.

Steve Carlton (for more information, see pages 36–37)

Year	Team	W	L	G	GS	CG	SV	IP	BB	SO	ERA
1965	St. Louis	0	0	15	2	0	0	25.0	8	21	2.52
1966	St. Louis	3	3	9	9	2	0	52.0	18	25	3.12
1967	St. Louis	14	9	30	28	11	1	193.0	62	168	2.98
1968	St. Louis	13	11	34	33	10	0	231.2	61	162	2.99
1969	St. Louis	17	11	31	31	12	0	236.1	93	210	2.17
1970	St. Louis	10	**19**	34	33	13	0	253.2	109	193	3.73
1971	St. Louis	20	9	37	36	18	0	273.1	98	172	3.56
1972	Philadelphia	**27**	10	41	**41**	**30**	0	**346.1**	87	**310**	**1.97**
1973	Philadelphia	13	**20**	40	**40**	18	0	**293.1**	113	223	3.90
1974	Philadelphia	16	13	39	39	17	0	291.0	**136**	**240**	3.22
1975	Philadelphia	15	14	37	37	14	0	255.1	104	192	3.56
1976	Philadelphia	20	7	35	35	13	0	252.2	72	195	3.13
1977	Philadelphia	**23**	10	36	36	17	0	283.0	89	198	2.64
1978	Philadelphia	16	13	34	34	12	0	247.1	63	161	2.84
1979	Philadelphia	18	11	35	35	13	0	251.0	89	213	3.62
1980	Philadelphia	**24**	9	38	**38**	13	0	**304.0**	90	**286**	2.34
1981	Philadelphia	13	4	24	24	10	0	190.0	62	179	2.42
1982	Philadelphia	**23**	11	38	**38**	19	0	**295.2**	86	**286**	3.10
1983	Philadelphia	15	16	37	37	8	0	**283.2**	84	**275**	3.11
1984	Philadelphia	13	7	33	33	1	0	229.0	79	163	3.58
1985	Philadelphia	1	8	16	16	0	0	92.0	53	48	3.33
1986	Philadelphia	4	8	16	16	0	0	83.0	45	62	6.18
1986	Chi. White Sox	4	3	10	10	0	0	63.1	25	40	3.69
1986	San Francisco	1	3	6	6	0	0	30.0	16	18	5.10
1987	Cleveland	5	9	23	14	3	1	109.0	63	71	5.37
1987	Minnesota	1	5	9	7	0	0	43.0	23	20	6.70
1988	Minnesota	0	1	4	1	0	0	9.2	5	5	16.76
Totals		**329**	**244**	**741**	**709**	**254**	**2**	**5217.1**	**1833**	**4136**	**3.22**

Bold = Led league

Notes
>Inducted into the Hall of Fame in his first year of eligibility in 1994;
>Ten-time All-Star (1968–1969, 1971–1972, 1974, 1977, 1979–1982);
>Appeared in the postseason in eight years, and went 2-2 with a 2.56 ERA in six games during four World Series (1967–1968, 1980, 1983).

Roger Clemens (for more information, see pages 38–39)

Year	Team	W	L	G	GS	CG	SV	IP	BB	SO	ERA
1984	Boston	9	4	21	20	5	0	133.1	29	126	4.32
1985	Boston	7	5	15	15	3	0	98.1	37	74	3.29
1986	Boston	**24**	4	33	33	10	0	254.0	67	238	**2.48**
1987	Boston	**20**	9	36	36	**18**	0	281.2	83	256	2.97
1988	Boston	18	12	35	35	**14**	0	264.0	62	**291**	2.93
1989	Boston	17	11	35	35	8	0	253.1	93	230	3.13
1990	Boston	21	6	31	31	7	0	228.1	54	209	**1.93**
1991	Boston	18	10	35	**35**	13	0	**271.1**	65	**241**	**2.62**
1992	Boston	18	11	32	32	11	0	246.2	62	208	**2.41**
1993	Boston	11	14	29	29	2	0	191.2	67	160	4.46
1994	Boston	9	7	24	24	3	0	170.2	71	168	2.85
1995	Boston	10	5	23	23	0	0	140.0	60	132	4.18
1996	Boston	10	13	34	34	6	0	242.2	106	**257**	3.63
1997	Toronto	**21**	7	34	34	**9**	0	**264.0**	68	**292**	**2.05**
1998	Toronto	**20**	6	33	33	5	0	234.2	88	**271**	**2.65**
1999	N.Y. Yankees	14	10	30	30	1	0	187.2	90	163	4.60
2000	N.Y. Yankees	13	8	32	32	1	0	204.1	84	188	3.70
2001	N.Y. Yankees	20	3	33	33	0	0	220.1	72	213	3.51
2002	N.Y. Yankees	13	6	29	29	0	0	180.0	63	192	4.35
2003	N.Y. Yankees	17	9	33	33	1	0	211.2	58	190	3.91
Totals		**310**	**160**	**607**	**606**	**117**	**0**	**4278.2**	**1379**	**4099**	**3.19**

Bold = Led league

Notes
>Nine-time All-Star (1986, 1988, 1990–1992, 1997, 1998, 2001, and 2002);
>Appeared in postseason play eight times, including five World Series (1986, 1999, 2000, 2001, 2003), posting a 2-2 record, 1.90 ERA, and 48 strikeouts and just 45 baserunners in 47.1 innings pitched in 7 career games;
>Won Cy Young Award a record six times (1986, 1987, 1991, 1997, 1998, and 2001);
>Is one of six pitchers to win consecutive Cy Young Awards (Sandy Koufax, Denny McLain, Jim Palmer, Pedro Martinez, and Randy Johnson are the others);
>Also won American League Most Valuable Player award in 1986;
>First pitcher to strike out 20 batters in a nine-inning game (April 29, 1986) and the only pitcher to do it twice (striking out 20 again on September 18, 1996);
>Third all-time in strikeouts, trailing Nolan Ryan and Steve Carlton;
>Won American League record 20 consecutive games (June 3, 1998–June 1, 1999);
>Third-best winning percentage (.659) among 300-game winners.

David Cone (for more information, see pages 8–9)

Year	Team	W	L	G	GS	CG	SV	IP	BB	SO	ERA
1986	Kansas City	0	0	11	0	0	0	22.2	13	21	5.56
1987	N.Y. Mets	5	6	21	13	1	1	99.1	44	68	3.71
1988	N.Y. Mets	20	3	35	28	8	0	231.1	80	213	2.22
1989	N.Y. Mets	14	8	34	33	7	0	219.2	74	190	3.52
1990	N.Y. Mets	14	10	31	30	6	0	211.2	65	**233**	3.23
1991	N.Y. Mets	14	14	34	34	5	0	232.2	73	**241**	3.29
1992	N.Y. Mets	13	7	27	27	7	0	196.2	**82**	214	2.88
1992	Toronto	4	3	8	7	0	0	53.0	29	47	2.55
1993	Kansas City	11	14	34	34	6	0	254.0	114	191	3.33
1994	Kansas City	16	5	23	23	4	0	171.2	54	132	2.94
1995	Toronto	9	6	17	17	5	0	**130.1**	41	102	3.38
1995	N.Y. Yankees	9	2	13	13	1	0	**99.0**	47	89	3.82
1996	N.Y. Yankees	7	2	11	11	1	0	72.0	34	71	2.88
1997	N.Y. Yankees	12	6	29	29	1	0	195.0	86	222	2.82
1998	N.Y. Yankees	**20**	7	31	31	3	0	207.2	59	209	3.55
1999	N.Y. Yankees	12	9	31	31	1	0	193.1	90	177	3.44
2000	N.Y. Yankees	4	14	30	29	0	0	155.0	82	120	6.91
2001	Boston	9	7	25	25	0	0	135.2	57	115	4.31
2003	N.Y. Mets	1	3	5	4	0	0	18.0	13	13	6.50
Totals		**194**	**126**	**450**	**419**	**56**	**1**	**2898.2**	**1137**	**2668**	**3.46**

Bold = Led league

Notes
>Five-time All-Star (1988, 1992, 1994, 1997, and 1999);
>Pitched in postseason play eight times, including five World Series (1992, 1996, 1998, 1999, and 2000) in which he went 2-0 with a 2.12 ERA in 6 games;
>American League Cy Young Award winner (1994);
>Hurled perfect game against Montreal (July 18, 1999), the first perfect game in the history of interleague play;
>Hurled 3 complete-game one-hitters in his career prior to the perfect game;
>Struck out a career-high 19 hitters at Philadelphia (October 6, 1991);
>In 1988, led National League in winning percentage (.870), which is the sixth-best mark ever for a 20-game winner;
>Sat out 2002 season, and made comeback with Mets in 2003 before retiring;
>The Mets originally acquired Cone from the Royals in a deal in which the most successful of the three players traded to Kansas City, catcher Ed Hearn, had just 35 at-bats in two seasons with the Royals.

Dizzy Dean (for more information, see pages 62–63)

Year	Team	W	L	G	GS	CG	SV	IP	BB	SO	ERA
1930	St. Louis	1	0	1	1	1	0	9.0	3	5	1.00
1932	St. Louis	18	15	46	33	16	2	**286.0**	102	**191**	3.30
1933	St. Louis	20	18	**48**	34	**26**	4	293.0	64	**199**	3.04
1934	St. Louis	**30**	7	50	33	24	7	311.2	75	**195**	2.66
1935	St. Louis	**28**	12	50	**36**	29	5	**325.1**	77	**190**	3.04
1936	St. Louis	24	13	**51**	34	**28**	11	**315.0**	53	195	3.17
1937	St. Louis	13	10	27	25	17	1	197.1	33	120	2.69
1938	Chicago Cubs	7	1	13	10	3	0	74.2	8	22	1.81
1939	Chicago Cubs	6	4	19	13	7	0	96.1	17	27	3.36
1940	Chicago Cubs	3	3	10	9	3	0	54.0	20	18	5.17
1941	Chicago Cubs	0	0	1	1	0	0	1.0	0	1	18.00
1947	St. Louis Browns	0	0	1	1	0	0	4.0	1	0	0.00
Totals		**150**	**83**	**317**	**230**	**154**	**30**	**1967.1**	**453**	**1163**	**3.02**

Bold = Led league

Notes
> Inducted into the Hall of Fame in 1953;
> Four-time All-Star (1934–1937);
> Appeared in two World Series (1934, 1938), posting a 2-2 record and a 2.88 ERA, including a 2-1 record and a 1.73 ERA in 26 innings as the Cardinals won the 1934 World Series;
> Won 1934 N.L. MVP award, and finished second in 1935 and 1936;
> Game's most dominant pitcher from 1932–1936: for each year during that five-year period he ranked among the top four in wins, top three in innings pitched, and top two in strikeouts;
> Last pitcher to record at least 20 wins and 10 saves in a season (1936);
> Was having another stellar season in 1937 when a line drive broke his toe while pitching in the All-Star Game. Dizzy attempted to come back too soon from the broken toe and injured his arm, leading to his rapid decline;
> Dizzy, so dubbed by an army sergeant, was known for his zany antics and bragging. When Dizzy threw a three-hit shutout in the opening game of a doubleheader but his brother hurled a no-hitter in the nightcap, Dizzy said, "I wished I'd a known Paul was goin' to pitch a no-hitter. I'd a pitched one, too."
> Dizzy had little schooling but became a broadcaster after his playing days—he drove grammar-school English teachers crazy by butchering the language during his 20-plus years in the booth.

Don Drysdale (for more information, see pages 40–41)

Year	Team	W	L	G	GS	CG	SV	IP	BB	SO	ERA
1956	Brooklyn	5	5	25	12	2	0	99.0	31	55	2.64
1957	Brooklyn	17	9	34	29	9	0	221.0	61	148	2.69
1958	Los Angeles	12	13	44	29	6	0	211.2	72	131	4.17
1959	Los Angeles	17	13	44	36	15	2	270.2	93	**242**	3.46
1960	Los Angeles	15	14	41	36	15	2	269.0	72	**246**	2.84
1961	Los Angeles	13	10	40	37	10	0	244.0	83	182	3.69
1962	Los Angeles	**25**	9	43	**41**	19	1	**314.1**	78	**232**	2.83
1963	Los Angeles	19	17	42	**42**	17	0	315.1	57	251	2.63
1964	Los Angeles	18	16	40	**40**	21	0	**321.1**	68	237	2.18
1965	Los Angeles	23	12	44	**42**	20	1	308.1	66	210	2.77
1966	Los Angeles	13	16	40	40	11	0	273.2	45	177	3.42
1967	Los Angeles	13	16	38	38	9	0	282.0	60	196	2.74
1968	Los Angeles	14	12	31	31	12	0	239.0	56	155	2.15
1969	Los Angeles	5	4	12	12	1	0	62.2	13	24	4.45
Totals		**209**	**166**	**518**	**465**	**167**	**6**	**3432.0**	**855**	**2486**	**2.95**

Bold = Led league

Notes

>Inducted into the Hall of Fame in 1984;

>Eight-time All Star (1959, 1961–1965, 1967–1968);

>Pitched in the World Series five times, posting a 3-3 record and a 2.95 ERA with 36 strikeouts in 39.2 innings pitched;

>Won the 1962 Cy Young Award;

>Set record with 58.2 scoreless innings (1968) and holds the record with 6 consecutive shutouts;

>A true workhorse, Don is the only pitcher since 1900 to start at least 40 games in five consecutive seasons (1962–1966), and he ranked in the top ten in both innings pitched and strikeouts for 11 consecutive seasons (1957–1967);

>N.L. record-holder for most seasons leading the league in hit batters (5). His philosophy on pitching inside: "If one of our guys went down, I just doubled it. No confusion there.";

>Hit 29 career home runs, second best by a pitcher in N.L. history;

>Hit .300 and won 20 games in the same season (1965);

>Owns the record for longest career played under one manager (Walter Alston), who was Drysdale's manager for his entire 14-year career.

Dennis Eckersley (for more information, see pages 102–103)

Year	Team	W	L	G	GS	CG	SV	IP	BB	SO	ERA
1975	Cleveland	13	7	34	24	6	2	186.2	90	152	2.60
1976	Cleveland	13	12	36	30	9	1	199.1	78	200	3.43
1977	Cleveland	14	13	33	33	12	0	247.1	54	191	3.53
1978	Boston	20	8	35	35	16	0	268.1	71	162	2.99
1979	Boston	17	10	33	33	17	0	246.1	59	150	2.99
1980	Boston	12	14	30	30	8	0	197.2	44	121	4.28
1981	Boston	9	8	23	23	8	0	154.0	35	79	4.27
1982	Boston	13	13	33	33	11	0	224.1	43	127	3.73
1983	Boston	9	13	28	28	2	0	176.1	39	77	5.61
1984	Boston	4	4	9	9	2	0	64.2	13	33	5.01
1984	Chicago Cubs	10	8	24	24	2	0	160.1	36	81	3.03
1985	Chicago Cubs	11	7	25	25	6	0	169.1	19	117	3.08
1986	Chicago Cubs	6	11	33	32	1	0	201.0	43	137	4.57
1987	Oakland	6	8	54	2	0	16	115.2	17	113	3.03
1988	Oakland	4	2	60	0	0	**45**	72.2	11	70	2.35
1989	Oakland	4	0	51	0	0	33	57.2	3	55	1.56
1990	Oakland	4	2	63	0	0	48	73.1	4	73	0.61
1991	Oakland	5	4	67	0	0	43	76.0	9	87	2.96
1992	Oakland	7	1	69	0	0	**51**	80.0	11	93	1.91
1993	Oakland	2	4	64	0	0	36	67.0	13	80	4.16
1994	Oakland	5	4	45	0	0	19	44.1	13	47	4.26
1995	Oakland	4	6	52	0	0	29	50.1	11	40	4.83
1996	St. Louis	0	6	63	0	0	30	60.0	6	49	3.30
1997	St. Louis	1	5	57	0	0	36	53.0	8	45	3.91
1998	Boston	4	1	50	0	0	1	39.2	8	22	4.76
Totals		**197**	**171**	**1071**	**361**	**100**	**390**	**3285.2**	**738**	**2401**	**3.50**

Bold = Led league

Notes
>Six-time All-Star (1977, 1982, 1988, 1990–1992);
>Pitched in postseason play seven times, including in three consecutive World Series from 1988–1990);
>Won both the Cy Young and Most Valuable Player awards in 1992;
>Hurled a no-hitter for Cleveland against California on May 30, 1977;
>Second all-time in games pitched (behind Jesse Orosco);
>Third all-time in saves (behind Lee Smith and John Franco);
>From 1988–1992, he was 24-9 with 220 saves and a 1.90 ERA.

Bob Feller (for more information, see pages 42–43)

Year	Team	W	L	G	GS	CG	SV	IP	BB	SO	ERA
1936	Cleveland	5	3	14	8	5	1	62.0	47	76	3.34
1937	Cleveland	9	7	26	19	9	1	148.2	106	150	3.39
1938	Cleveland	17	11	39	36	20	1	277.2	**208**	**240**	4.08
1939	Cleveland	**24**	9	39	35	**24**	1	**296.2**	142	246	2.85
1940	Cleveland	**27**	11	**43**	37	**31**	4	**320.1**	118	**261**	**2.61**
1941	Cleveland	**25**	13	**44**	**40**	28	2	**343.0**	194	260	3.15
1945	Cleveland	5	3	9	9	7	0	72.0	35	59	2.50
1946	Cleveland	**26**	15	**48**	42	**36**	4	**371.1**	153	**348**	2.18
1947	Cleveland	**20**	11	42	**37**	20	3	**299.0**	127	**196**	2.68
1948	Cleveland	19	15	44	**38**	18	3	280.1	116	**164**	3.56
1949	Cleveland	15	14	36	28	15	0	211.0	84	108	3.75
1950	Cleveland	16	11	35	34	16	0	247.0	103	119	3.43
1951	Cleveland	**22**	8	33	32	16	0	249.2	95	111	3.50
1952	Cleveland	9	13	30	30	11	0	191.2	83	81	4.74
1953	Cleveland	10	7	25	25	10	0	175.2	60	60	3.59
1954	Cleveland	13	3	19	19	9	0	140.0	39	59	3.09
1955	Cleveland	4	4	25	11	2	0	83.0	31	25	3.47
1956	Cleveland	0	4	19	4	2	1	58.0	23	18	4.97
Totals		**266**	**162**	**570**	**484**	**279**	**21**	**3827.0**	**1764**	**2581**	**3.25**

Bold = Led league

Notes

>First-ballot Hall of Fame inductee in 1962;
>Eight-time All-Star (1938–1941, 1946–1948, 1950);
>Pitched in one World Series (1948), posting an 0-2 record and a 5.02 ERA;
>Won A.L.'s unofficial pitching Triple Crown in 1940 (he led the league in wins, strikeouts, and ERA);
>Only pitcher to hurl a no-hitter on Opening Day (at Chicago in 1940);
>Struck out 15 in his first start and 17 in his fifth start as a 17-year-old in 1936— and when the season ended, he returned to his senior year of high school;
>One of three pitchers with 1,000 strikeouts before age 24 (joining Bert Blyleven and Dwight Gooden);
>Won 107 games before age 23;
>Shares A.L. record for most seasons leading the league in starts (5, with Early Wynn);
>Set dubious Major League post-1900 record for walks in a season (208 in 1938);

Rollie Fingers (for more information, see pages 104–105)

Year	Team	W	L	G	GS	CG	SV	IP	BB	SO	ERA
1968	Oakland	0	0	1	0	0	0	1.1	1	0	27.00
1969	Oakland	6	7	60	8	1	12	119.0	41	61	3.71
1970	Oakland	7	9	45	19	1	2	148.0	48	79	3.65
1971	Oakland	4	6	48	8	2	17	129.1	30	98	2.99
1972	Oakland	11	9	65	0	0	21	111.1	32	113	2.51
1973	Oakland	7	8	62	2	0	22	126.2	39	110	1.92
1974	Oakland	9	5	**76**	0	0	18	119.0	29	95	2.65
1975	Oakland	10	6	**75**	0	0	24	126.2	33	115	2.98
1976	Oakland	13	11	70	0	0	20	134.2	40	113	2.47
1977	San Diego	8	9	**78**	0	0	**35**	132.1	36	113	2.99
1978	San Diego	6	13	67	0	0	**37**	107.1	29	72	2.52
1979	San Diego	9	9	54	0	0	13	83.2	37	65	4.52
1980	San Diego	11	9	66	0	0	23	103.0	32	69	2.80
1981	Milwaukee	6	3	47	0	0	**28**	78.0	13	61	1.04
1982	Milwaukee	5	6	50	0	0	29	79.2	20	71	2.60
1984	Milwaukee	1	2	33	0	0	23	46.0	13	40	1.96
1985	Milwaukee	1	6	47	0	0	17	55.1	19	24	5.04
Totals		**114**	**118**	**944**	**37**	**4**	**341**	**1701.1**	**492**	**1299**	**2.90**

Bold = Led league

Notes
> Inducted into the Baseball Hall of Fame in 1992;
> Seven-time All Star (1973–1976, 1978, 1981–1982);
> Pitched in postseason play six times, including three consecutive World Series from 1972–1974;
> Pitched in 16 of the 19 World Series games from 1972–1974, posting two wins, six saves, and a 1.35 ERA in 33.1 innings to help the Oakland A's win all three championships;
> Ranked in the top two in games pitched six consecutive seasons (1972–1977), and finished in the top four in saves 11 times in a 12-year span (1971–1982);
> Signed with San Diego as a free agent in 1977, and was part of an 11-player trade from San Diego to St. Louis in 1981;
> Missed the end of the 1982 season (including the Brewers' only World Series appearance) and all of the 1983 season with an arm injury, but bounced back at age 38 in 1984 to save 23 games with a 1.96 ERA.

Whitey Ford (for more information, see pages 88–89)

Year	Team	W	L	G	GS	CG	SV	IP	BB	SO	ERA
1950	N.Y. Yankees	9	1	20	12	7	1	112.0	52	59	2.81
1953	N.Y. Yankees	18	6	32	30	11	0	207.0	110	110	3.00
1954	N.Y. Yankees	16	8	34	28	11	1	210.2	101	125	2.82
1955	N.Y. Yankees	**18**	7	39	33	**18**	2	253.2	113	137	2.63
1956	N.Y. Yankees	19	6	31	30	18	1	225.2	84	141	**2.47**
1957	N.Y. Yankees	11	5	24	17	5	0	129.1	53	84	2.57
1958	N.Y. Yankees	14	7	30	29	15	1	219.1	62	145	**2.01**
1959	N.Y. Yankees	16	10	35	29	9	1	204.0	89	114	3.04
1960	N.Y. Yankees	12	9	33	29	8	0	192.2	65	85	3.08
1961	N.Y. Yankees	**25**	4	39	**39**	11	0	**283.0**	92	209	3.21
1962	N.Y. Yankees	17	8	38	37	7	0	257.2	69	160	2.90
1963	N.Y. Yankees	**24**	7	38	**37**	13	1	**269.1**	56	189	2.74
1964	N.Y. Yankees	17	6	39	36	12	1	244.2	57	172	2.13
1965	N.Y. Yankees	16	13	37	36	9	1	244.1	50	162	3.24
1966	N.Y. Yankees	2	5	22	9	0	0	73.0	24	43	2.47
1967	N.Y. Yankees	2	4	7	7	2	0	44.0	9	21	1.64
Totals		**236**	**106**	**498**	**438**	**156**	**10**	**3170.1**	**1086**	**1956**	**2.75**

Bold = Led league

Notes

>Inducted into the Baseball Hall of Fame in 1974;
>Eight-time All Star (1954–1956, 1958–1961, 1964);
>Pitched in 11 World Series, and owns records for wins (10), games started (22), opening-games started (8), consecutive scoreless innings (33), most innings (146), and strikeouts (94);
>He was named the 1961 World Series MVP after throwing 14 shutout innings and winning both of his starts;
>Owns the highest career winning percentage (.690) of any pitcher with at least 200 career victories;
>Ranked among the A.L.'s top three in ERA five times;
>Twice led the league in shutouts (1958, 1960);
>Through the 1960 season, when Casey Stengel was his manager, Whitey often was rested four days between starts. When Ralph Houk became manager in 1961, Ford was put in a four-man rotation and had his Cy Young-winning year;
>Nicknamed "Chairman of the Board" for his businesslike approach to the game;
>Missed 1951 and 1952 seasons while serving in the Korean War.

Eric Gagné (for more information, see pages 106–107)

Year	Team	W	L	G	GS	CG	SV	IP	BB	SO	ERA
1999	Los Angeles	1	1	5	5	0	0	30.0	15	30	2.10
2000	Los Angeles	4	6	20	19	0	0	101.1	60	79	5.15
2001	Los Angeles	6	7	33	24	0	0	151.2	46	130	4.75
2002	Los Angeles	4	1	77	0	0	52	82.1	16	114	1.97
2003	Los Angeles	2	3	77	0	0	**55**	82.1	20	137	1.20
Totals		**17**	**18**	**212**	**48**	**0**	**107**	**447.2**	**157**	**490**	**3.50**

Bold = Led league

Notes
>Two-time All-Star (2002–2003);
>Finished fourth in the N.L. Cy Young award voting in 2002;
>Won 2003 N.L. Cy Young award; first reliever to win since 1989;
>First reliever to post two 50-save seasons, and he did it consecutively (2002–2003);
>After just two seasons as a closer, owns two of the top six single-season marks for saves (55 in 2003 and 52 in 2002);
>Set a record by converting 100 percent of his save chances in a season (55 for 55 in 2003);
>Established a record with 63 consecutive save conversions through end of 2003;
>Struck out a single-season record 14.98 hitters per nine innings in 2003;
>In 2003, became first reliever to have at least 100 more strikeouts than hits allowed (137 strikeouts compared to 37 hits allowed);
>Of his 55 saves in 2003, 24 of them protected a one-run lead;
>Allowed just one run after the All-Star break in 2003 (37 innings, for a 0.24 ERA);
>In 2002, he set records for fewest number of his team's games to reach 20 saves (game number 56) and 30 saves (game number 82);
>In his first two seasons as closer (2002–2003), he has a 1.58 ERA and has struck out 251 batters (13.75 per nine innings) with only 36 walks;
>Born in Canada, he grew up within walking distance of the Montreal Expos' Olympic Stadium;
>Of French-speaking descent, did not learn to speak English until he attended Seminole State Junior College in Oklahoma;
>While recovering from elbow surgery in 1997, he contemplated retiring from baseball and accepting a hockey scholarship from the University of Vermont;
>Wears protective goggles while pitching because of an old hockey injury.

Bob Gibson (for more information, see pages 90–91)

Year	Team	W	L	G	GS	CG	SV	IP	BB	SO	ERA
1959	St. Louis	3	5	13	9	2	0	75.2	39	48	3.33
1960	St. Louis	3	6	27	12	2	0	86.2	48	69	5.61
1961	St. Louis	13	12	35	27	10	1	211.1	**119**	166	3.24
1962	St. Louis	15	13	32	30	15	1	233.2	95	208	2.85
1963	St. Louis	18	9	36	33	14	0	254.2	96	204	3.39
1964	St. Louis	19	12	40	36	17	1	287.1	86	245	3.01
1965	St. Louis	20	12	38	36	20	1	299.0	103	270	3.07
1966	St. Louis	21	12	35	35	20	0	280.1	78	225	2.44
1967	St. Louis	13	7	24	24	10	0	175.1	40	147	2.98
1968	St. Louis	22	9	34	34	28	0	304.2	62	**268**	**1.12**
1969	St. Louis	20	13	35	35	**28**	0	314.0	95	269	2.18
1970	St. Louis	**23**	7	34	34	23	0	294.0	88	274	3.12
1971	St. Louis	16	13	31	31	20	0	245.2	76	185	3.04
1972	St. Louis	19	11	34	34	23	0	278.0	88	208	2.46
1973	St. Louis	12	10	25	25	13	0	195.0	57	142	2.77
1974	St. Louis	11	13	33	33	9	0	240.0	104	129	3.83
1975	St. Louis	3	10	22	14	1	2	109.0	62	60	5.04
Totals		**251**	**174**	**528**	**482**	**255**	**6**	**3884.1**	**1336**	**3117**	**2.91**

Bold = Led league

Notes

>First-ballot Hall of Fame inductee in 1981;
>Eight-time All-Star (1962, 1965–1970, 1972);
>Pitched in three World Series (1964, 1967–68), completing eight of nine starts and posting a 7-2 record with 92 strikeouts in 81 innings;
>Was the MVP of the Cardinals' 1964 and 1967 World Series teams, when he won the series-clinching game both times;
>Struck out a World Series-record 17 batters in Game 1 in 1968, and set a single-series record with 35 strikeouts that year;
>Two-time N.L. Cy Young Award winner (1968 and 1970);
>Also won N.L. Most Valuable Player award in 1968;
>Won nine consecutive N.L. Gold Glove awards from 1965–1973;
>Hurled a no-hitter at Pittsburgh on August 14, 1971;
>A tremendous athlete, he played one year with basketball's Harlem Globetrotters and could jump and touch the basketball rim with his elbow.

Tom Glavine (for more information, see pages 10–11)

Year	Team	W	L	G	GS	CG	SV	IP	BB	SO	ERA
1987	Atlanta	2	4	9	9	0	0	50.1	33	20	5.54
1988	Atlanta	7	**17**	34	34	1	0	195.1	63	84	4.56
1989	Atlanta	14	8	29	29	6	0	186.0	40	90	3.68
1990	Atlanta	10	12	33	33	1	0	214.1	78	129	4.28
1991	Atlanta	**20**	11	34	34	**9**	0	246.2	69	192	2.55
1992	Atlanta	**20**	8	33	33	7	0	225.0	70	129	2.76
1993	Atlanta	**22**	6	36	**36**	4	0	239.1	90	120	3.20
1994	Atlanta	13	9	25	25	2	0	165.1	70	140	3.97
1995	Atlanta	16	7	29	29	3	0	198.2	66	127	3.08
1996	Atlanta	15	10	36	**36**	1	0	235.1	85	181	2.98
1997	Atlanta	14	7	33	33	5	0	240.0	79	152	2.96
1998	Atlanta	**20**	6	33	33	4	0	229.1	74	157	2.47
1999	Atlanta	14	11	35	**35**	2	0	234.0	83	138	4.12
2000	Atlanta	**21**	9	35	**35**	4	0	241.0	65	152	3.40
2001	Atlanta	16	7	35	**35**	1	0	219.1	97	116	3.57
2002	Atlanta	18	11	36	**36**	2	0	224.2	78	127	2.96
2003	N.Y. Mets	9	14	32	32	0	0	183.1	66	82	4.52
Totals		**251**	**157**	**537**	**537**	**52**	**0**	**3528.0**	**1206**	**2136**	**3.43**

Bold = Led league

Notes
> Eight-time All-Star (1991–1993, 1996–1998, 2000, 2002);
> Pitched in postseason play 11 times, including five World Series (1991–1992, 1995–1996, and 1999);
> Posted a 4-3 record with a 2.16 ERA in eight World Series games, and was 2-0 with a 1.29 ERA to earn 1995 World Series MVP honors;
> A two-time N.L. Cy Young award winner (1991 and 1998) who finished in the top three in voting a total of six times;
> In 1998, he led the N.L. in wins (20), was second in winning percentage (.769), and was fourth in ERA (2.47) and shutouts (three);
> Ranks ninth all-time in victories among lefthanders (251);
> Is the 33rd pitcher since 1900 to win at least 20 games in a season five times;
> From 1991–1996, was the winningest pitcher in baseball (106 victories);
> Ranked in the top eight in the league in ERA eight times.

Lefty Grove (for more information, see pages 64–65)

Year	Team	W	L	G	GS	CG	SV	IP	BB	SO	ERA
1925	Phil. Athletics	10	12	45	18	5	1	197.0	**131**	**116**	4.75
1926	Phil. Athletics	13	13	45	33	20	6	258.0	101	**194**	2.51
1927	Phil. Athletics	20	13	51	28	14	9	262.1	79	**174**	3.19
1928	Phil. Athletics	**24**	8	39	31	24	4	261.2	64	**183**	2.58
1929	Phil. Athletics	20	6	42	**37**	19	4	275.1	81	**170**	2.81
1930	Phil. Athletics	**28**	5	**50**	32	22	**9**	291.0	60	**209**	2.54
1931	Phil. Athletics	**31**	4	41	30	**27**	5	288.2	62	**175**	2.06
1932	Phil. Athletics	25	10	44	30	**27**	7	291.2	79	188	2.84
1933	Phil. Athletics	**24**	8	45	28	**21**	6	275.1	83	114	3.20
1934	Boston	8	8	22	12	5	0	109.1	32	43	6.50
1935	Boston	20	12	35	30	23	1	273.0	65	121	**2.70**
1936	Boston	17	12	35	30	22	2	253.1	65	130	**2.81**
1937	Boston	17	9	32	32	21	0	262.0	83	153	3.02
1938	Boston	14	4	24	21	12	1	163.2	52	99	**3.08**
1939	Boston	15	4	23	23	17	0	191.0	58	81	**2.54**
1940	Boston	7	6	22	21	9	0	153.1	50	62	3.99
1941	Boston	7	7	21	21	10	0	134.0	42	54	4.37
Totals		**300**	**141**	**616**	**457**	**298**	**55**	**3940.2**	**1187**	**2266**	**3.06**

Bold = Led league

Notes
>Hall of Fame inductee in 1947;
>Selected to six of the first seven All-Star Games (1933, 1935–1939);
>Pitched in three World Series (1929–1931), posting a 4-2 record, 2 saves, and a 1.75 ERA in eight games;
>A.L. Most Valuable Player in 1931, when he went 31-4 and established a record for best winning percentage in a season (.886);
>Has the best career winning percentage (.680) of the 21 Major League pitchers who have won 300 games;
>Led the A.L. in ERA a record nine times—no other pitcher has led his league in ERA more than five times;
>Lefty and Sandy Koufax are the only pitchers to twice strike out the side on only nine pitches;
>The Athletics paid the International League's Baltimore Orioles a record $100,600 for Lefty, surpassing the $100,000 fee the Red Sox paid the same minor-league team for Babe Ruth.

Orel Hershiser (for more information, see pages 92–93)

Year	Team	W	L	G	GS	CG	SV	IP	BB	SO	ERA
1983	Los Angeles	0	0	8	0	0	1	8.0	6	5	3.38
1984	Los Angeles	11	8	45	20	8	2	189.2	50	150	2.66
1985	Los Angeles	19	3	36	34	9	0	239.2	68	157	2.03
1986	Los Angeles	14	14	35	35	8	0	231.1	86	153	3.85
1987	Los Angeles	16	16	37	35	10	1	**264.2**	74	190	3.06
1988	Los Angeles	**23**	8	35	34	**15**	1	**267.0**	73	178	2.26
1989	Los Angeles	15	**15**	35	33	8	0	**256.2**	77	178	2.31
1990	Los Angeles	1	1	4	4	0	0	25.1	4	16	4.26
1991	Los Angeles	7	2	21	21	0	0	112.0	32	73	3.46
1992	Los Angeles	10	**15**	33	33	1	0	210.2	69	130	3.67
1993	Los Angeles	12	14	33	33	5	0	215.2	72	141	3.59
1994	Los Angeles	6	6	21	21	1	0	135.1	42	72	3.79
1995	Cleveland	16	6	26	26	1	0	167.1	51	111	3.87
1996	Cleveland	15	9	33	33	1	0	206.0	58	125	4.24
1997	Cleveland	14	6	32	32	1	0	195.1	69	107	4.47
1998	San Francisco	11	10	34	34	0	0	202.0	85	126	4.41
1999	N.Y. Mets	13	11	32	32	0	0	179.0	77	89	4.58
2000	Los Angeles	1	5	10	6	0	0	24.2	14	13	13.14
Totals		**204**	**149**	**510**	**466**	**68**	**5**	**3130.1**	**1007**	**2014**	**3.48**

Bold = Led league

Notes
>Three-time All-Star (1987–1989);
>Pitched in eight postseason series, and was named MVP in three of them: the 1988 World Series, 1988 NLCS, and 1995 ALCS;
>In the 1988 postseason, Orel was 1-0 with one save and a 1.09 ERA against the Mets in the NLCS, then went 2-0 with a 1.00 ERA and two complete games against Oakland in the World Series;
>Was 3-3 overall with a 4.07 ERA while pitching in three career World Series (1988, 1995, 1997);
>Went 3-for-3 at the plate, with two doubles, in the 1988 World Series;
>Won the 1988 N.L. Cy Young Award;
>Ranked second or third in the N.L. in ERA five times in his first six full seasons (1984–1989);
>Bounced back from an arm injury suffered in April 1990 to win 105 more games.

Carl Hubbell (for more information, see pages 12–13)

Year	Team	W	L	G	GS	CG	SV	IP	BB	SO	ERA
1928	N.Y. Giants	10	6	20	14	8	1	124.0	21	37	2.83
1929	N.Y. Giants	18	11	39	35	19	1	268.0	67	106	3.69
1930	N.Y. Giants	17	12	37	32	17	2	241.2	58	117	3.87
1931	N.Y. Giants	14	12	36	30	21	3	248.0	67	155	2.65
1932	N.Y. Giants	18	11	40	32	22	2	284.0	40	137	2.50
1933	N.Y. Giants	**23**	12	45	33	22	5	**308.2**	47	156	**1.66**
1934	N.Y. Giants	21	12	49	35	**25**	**8**	313.0	37	118	**2.30**
1935	N.Y. Giants	23	12	42	35	24	0	302.2	49	150	3.27
1936	N.Y. Giants	**26**	6	42	34	25	3	304.0	57	123	**2.31**
1937	N.Y. Giants	**22**	8	39	32	18	4	261.2	55	**159**	3.20
1938	N.Y. Giants	13	10	24	22	13	1	179.0	33	104	3.07
1939	N.Y. Giants	11	9	29	18	10	2	154.0	24	62	2.75
1940	N.Y. Giants	11	12	31	27	11	0	214.1	59	86	3.65
1941	N.Y. Giants	11	9	26	22	11	1	164.0	53	75	3.57
1942	N.Y. Giants	11	8	24	20	11	0	157.1	34	61	3.95
1943	N.Y. Giants	4	4	12	11	3	0	66.0	24	31	4.91
Totals		**253**	**154**	**535**	**431**	**260**	**33**	**3590.1**	**725**	**1677**	**2.98**

Bold = Led league

Notes
> Hall of Fame inductee in 1947;
> Nine-time All-Star (1933–1938, 1940–1942);
> Pitched in three World Series (1933, 1936–1937)
> He was 4-2 with a 1.79 ERA in six career World Series games, tossing a complete game in all four wins, including an 11-inning, 2-1 victory over the Washington Senators in Game 4 in 1933;
> Holds the record for consecutive scoreless innings by a lefthander (45.1 innings from July 13–August 1, 1933);
> Carl was signed by the Tigers in 1925, but Detroit manager Ty Cobb refused to let him throw his screwball. The New York Giants' John McGraw eventually signed him and let him throw the pitch at will.

Catfish Hunter (for more information, see pages 66–67)

Year	Team	W	L	G	GS	CG	SV	IP	BB	SO	ERA
1965	K.C. Athletics	8	8	32	20	3	0	133.0	46	82	4.26
1966	K.C. Athletics	9	11	30	25	4	0	176.2	64	103	4.02
1967	K.C. Athletics	13	17	35	35	13	0	259.2	84	196	2.81
1968	Oakland	13	13	36	34	11	1	234.0	69	172	3.35
1969	Oakland	12	15	38	35	10	0	247.0	85	150	3.35
1970	Oakland	18	14	40	**40**	9	0	262.1	74	178	3.81
1971	Oakland	21	11	37	37	16	0	273.2	80	181	2.96
1972	Oakland	21	7	38	37	16	0	295.1	70	191	2.04
1973	Oakland	21	5	36	36	11	0	256.1	69	124	3.34
1974	Oakland	**25**	12	41	41	23	0	318.1	46	143	**2.49**
1975	N.Y. Yankees	**23**	14	39	39	**30**	0	**328.0**	83	177	2.58
1976	N.Y. Yankees	17	15	36	36	21	0	298.2	68	173	3.53
1977	N.Y. Yankees	9	9	22	22	8	0	143.1	47	52	4.71
1978	N.Y. Yankees	12	6	21	20	5	0	118.0	35	56	3.58
1979	N.Y. Yankees	2	9	19	19	1	0	105.0	34	34	5.31
Totals		**224**	**166**	**500**	**476**	**181**	**1**	**3449.1**	**954**	**2012**	**3.26**

Bold = Led league

Notes
>Inducted into the Hall of Fame in 1987;
>Eight-time All-Star selection (1966–1967, 1970, 1972 1976);
>Pitched in postseason play seven times, including six World Series (1972–1974, 1976–1978) in which he went 5-3 with one save and a 3.29 ERA in 12 games;
>In World Series games with Oakland (1972–1974), he posted a 4-0 record with one save and a 2.19 ERA in seven appearances to help the A's win three consecutive championships;
>A.L. Cy Young Award winner in 1974, one of four consecutive seasons that he finished in the top four in the voting;
>Last pitcher to throw 30 complete games in a season (1975);
>Extremely durable, he did not miss a start from 1965–1977;
>Ranked among the A.L.'s top four in victories five consecutive seasons (1971–1975);
>Retired at age 33 because of arm strain and diabetes;
>Nicknamed "Catfish" by A's owner Charlie Finley purely for publicity—his given name was James.

Randy Johnson (for more information, see pages 44–45)

Year	Team	W	L	G	GS	CG	SV	IP	BB	SO	ERA
1988	Montreal	3	0	4	4	1	0	26.0	7	25	2.42
1989	Montreal	0	4	7	6	0	0	29.2	26	26	6.67
1989	Seattle	7	9	22	22	2	0	131.0	70	104	4.40
1990	Seattle	14	11	33	33	5	0	219.2	**120**	194	3.65
1991	Seattle	13	10	33	33	2	0	201.1	**152**	228	3.98
1992	Seattle	12	14	31	31	6	0	210.1	**144**	**241**	3.77
1993	Seattle	19	8	35	34	10	1	255.1	99	**308**	3.24
1994	Seattle	13	6	23	23	**9**	0	172.0	72	**204**	3.19
1995	Seattle	18	2	30	30	6	0	214.1	65	**294**	**2.48**
1996	Seattle	5	0	14	8	0	1	61.1	25	85	3.67
1997	Seattle	20	4	30	29	5	0	213.0	77	291	2.28
1998	Seattle	9	10	23	23	6	0	160.0	60	213	4.33
1998	Houston	10	1	11	11	4	0	84.1	26	116	1.28
1999	Arizona	17	9	35	**35**	**12**	0	**271.2**	70	364	**2.48**
2000	Arizona	19	7	35	**35**	**8**	0	248.2	76	347	2.64
2001	Arizona	21	6	35	34	3	0	249.2	71	372	**2.49**
2002	Arizona	**24**	5	35	35	**8**	0	**260.0**	71	334	**2.32**
2003	Arizona	6	8	18	18	1	0	114.0	27	125	4.26
Totals		**230**	**114**	**454**	**444**	**88**	**2**	**3122.1**	**1258**	**3871**	**3.10**

Bold = Led league

Notes

>Nine-time All-Star (1990, 1993–1995, 1997, 1999–2002);
>Pitched in postseason play six times, including one World Series (2001);
>He had a 1.04 ERA for Arizona in that 2001 Series against the Yankees and struck out 19 in 17.1 innings to share MVP honors with teammate Curt Schilling;
>Only the third pitcher to win the Cy Young Award in both the A.L. (1995) and the N.L. (1999–2002);
>Second pitcher to win four consecutive Cy Young Awards (joining Greg Maddux);
>Led the N.L. in wins, ERA, and strikeouts (the unofficial Triple Crown) in 2002;
>Hurled a no-hitter while pitching for Seattle against Detroit on June 2, 1990;
>Set a record with five consecutive 300-strikeout seasons (1998–2002) and ranks fourth in big-league history with 3,871 career strikeouts;
>Tied the Major League record by striking out 20 batters while pitching nine innings in a game on May 8, 2001, and set a record for strikeouts by a reliever with 16 (in seven innings) on July 19, 2001.

Walter Johnson (for more information, see pages 46–47)

Year	Team	W	L	G	GS	CG	SV	IP	BB	SO	ERA
1907	Washington	5	9	14	12	11	0	110.1	20	70	1.88
1908	Washington	14	14	36	30	23	1	256.1	53	160	1.65
1909	Washington	13	25	40	36	27	1	296.1	84	164	2.22
1910	Washington	25	17	**45**	**42**	**38**	1	**370.0**	76	**313**	1.36
1911	Washington	25	13	40	37	**36**	1	322.1	70	207	1.90
1912	Washington	33	12	50	37	34	2	369.0	76	**303**	**1.39**
1913	Washington	**36**	7	48	36	**29**	2	**346.0**	38	**243**	**1.14**
1914	Washington	**28**	18	**51**	**40**	**33**	1	**371.2**	74	**225**	1.72
1915	Washington	**27**	13	47	**39**	**35**	4	**336.2**	56	**203**	1.55
1916	Washington	**25**	20	48	38	**36**	1	**369.2**	82	**228**	1.90
1917	Washington	23	16	47	34	30	3	326.0	68	**188**	2.21
1918	Washington	**23**	13	39	29	29	3	326.0	70	**162**	**1.27**
1919	Washington	20	14	39	29	27	2	290.1	51	**147**	**1.49**
1920	Washington	8	10	21	15	12	3	143.2	27	78	3.13
1921	Washington	17	14	35	32	25	1	264.0	92	**143**	3.51
1922	Washington	15	16	41	31	23	4	280.0	99	105	2.99
1923	Washington	17	12	42	34	18	4	261.0	73	**130**	3.48
1924	Washington	**23**	7	38	**38**	20	0	277.2	77	**158**	**2.72**
1925	Washington	20	7	30	29	16	0	229.0	78	108	3.07
1926	Washington	15	16	33	33	22	0	260.2	73	125	3.63
1927	Washington	5	6	18	15	7	0	107.2	26	48	5.10
Totals		**417**	**279**	**802**	**666**	**531**	**34**	**5914.1**	**1363**	**3508**	**2.17**

Bold = Led league

Notes
>One of the five charter members elected to the Hall of Fame in 1936;
>Pitched in two career World Series (1924–1925), and posted a 3-3 record with a 2.16 ERA in six appearances;
>Two-time American League MVP (1913, 1924)
>Won pitching's unofficial Triple Crown (leading his league in wins, ERA, and strikeouts) in 1913, 1918, and 1924;
>Hurled a no-hitter against Boston at Fenway Park on July 1, 1920;
>Set A.L. record for consecutive scoreless innings (55.2 in 1913) and shares A.L. record for most consecutive victories in one season (16 in 1912);
>Owns the record for consecutive seasons leading league in strikeouts (eight from 1912–1919);
>Batted .235 with 24 career homers and was used as a pinch-hitter 132 times.

Sandy Koufax (for more information, see pages 48–49)

Year	Team	W	L	G	GS	CG	SV	IP	BB	SO	ERA
1955	Brooklyn	2	2	12	5	2	0	41.2	28	30	3.02
1956	Brooklyn	2	4	16	10	0	0	58.2	29	30	4.91
1957	Brooklyn	5	4	34	13	2	0	104.1	51	122	3.88
1958	Los Angeles	11	11	40	26	5	1	158.2	105	131	4.48
1959	Los Angeles	8	6	35	23	6	2	153.1	92	173	4.05
1960	Los Angeles	8	13	37	26	7	1	175.0	100	197	3.91
1961	Los Angeles	18	13	42	35	15	1	255.2	96	**269**	3.52
1962	Los Angeles	14	7	28	26	11	1	184.1	57	216	**2.54**
1963	Los Angeles	**25**	5	40	40	20	0	311.0	58	**306**	**1.88**
1964	Los Angeles	19	5	29	28	15	1	223.0	53	223	**1.74**
1965	Los Angeles	**26**	8	43	41	**27**	2	**335.2**	71	**382**	**2.04**
1966	Los Angeles	**27**	9	41	**41**	**27**	0	**323.0**	77	**317**	**1.73**
Totals		**165**	**87**	**397**	**314**	**137**	**9**	**2324.1**	**817**	**2396**	**2.76**

Bold = Led league

Notes

>At age 36 in 1972, he was the youngest Hall of Fame inductee in history;

>Six-time All-Star (1961–1966);

>Pitched in four World Series (1959, 1963, 1965–1966), posting a 4-3 record in eight games (seven starts) with a 0.95 ERA and 61 strikeouts in 57 innings;

>On two days' rest, shut out Minnesota while striking out 10 and allowing only three hits in Game 7 of the 1965 World Series;

>Won two World Series MVP awards (1963, 1965);

>Won three Major League Cy Young Awards (1963, 1965, 1966) and an N.L. MVP award (1963);

>Won pitching's unofficial Triple Crown (leading his league in wins, ERA, and strikeouts) in 1963, 1965, and 1966;

>Only pitcher to lead his league in ERA five consecutive seasons (1962–1966);

>Hurled N.L.-record four no-hitters (against the Mets at Dodger Stadium on June 30, 1962; against the Giants at Dodger Stadium on May 11, 1963; against the Phillies at Connie Mack Stadium on April 23, 1964; and a perfect game against the Cubs at Dodger Stadium on September 9, 1965);

>Set post-1900 single-season record for strikeouts (382 in 1965);

>Set N.L. record of eight games with at least 15 strikeouts, and 97 games with at least 10 strikeouts;

>His 11 shutouts in 1963 equals the second-most in a season since 1916.

Don Larsen (for more information, see pages 94–95)

Year	Team	W	L	G	GS	CG	SV	IP	BB	SO	ERA
1953	St. L. Browns	7	12	38	22	7	2	192.2	64	96	4.16
1954	Baltimore	3	**21**	29	28	12	0	201.2	89	80	4.37
1955	N.Y. Yankees	9	2	19	13	5	2	97.0	51	44	3.06
1956	N.Y. Yankees	11	5	38	20	6	1	179.2	96	107	3.26
1957	N.Y. Yankees	10	4	27	20	4	0	139.2	87	81	3.74
1958	N.Y. Yankees	9	6	19	19	5	0	114.1	52	55	3.07
1959	N.Y. Yankees	6	7	25	18	3	0	124.2	76	69	4.33
1960	K.C. Athletics	1	10	22	15	0	0	83.2	42	43	5.38
1961	K.C. Athletics	1	0	8	1	0	0	15.0	11	13	4.20
1961	Chi. White Sox	7	2	25	3	0	2	74.1	29	53	4.12
1962	San Francisco	5	4	49	0	0	11	86.1	47	58	4.38
1963	San Francisco	7	7	46	0	0	3	62.0	30	44	3.05
1964	San Francisco	0	1	6	0	0	0	10.1	6	6	4.35
1964	Houston	4	8	30	10	2	1	103.1	20	58	2.26
1965	Houston	0	0	1	1	0	0	5.1	3	1	5.06
1965	Baltimore	1	2	27	1	0	1	54.0	20	40	2.67
1967	Chicago Cubs	0	0	3	0	0	0	4.0	2	1	9.00
Totals		**81**	**91**	**412**	**171**	**44**	**26**	**1548.0**	**725**	**849**	**3.78**

Bold = Led league

Notes

> Pitched in five World Series (1955–1958, 1962) and posted a 4-2 record and a 2.75 ERA in 10 games, six of them starts;

> Was named the World Series MVP in 1956, the year of his perfect game against the Brooklyn Dodgers;

> Prior to his perfect game, Larsen had been knocked out of the second inning of Game 2, but Yankees manager Casey Stengel had a hunch and pitched him on two days' rest;

> Only won three games for Baltimore in 1954, and led the A.L. with 21 losses, but two of his victories came against the Yankees, and New York had him included in an 18-player deal prior to the 1955 season;

> Eventually moved to the bullpen, and was second on the team in saves (with 11) for the N.L.-champion Giants in 1962;

> A good hitter, he batted .242 with 14 home runs in his career;

> Was the last player active (1967) who had been a member of the Browns, which left St. Louis after the 1953 season.

Greg Maddux (for more information, see pages 68–69)

Year	Team	W	L	G	GS	CG	SV	IP	BB	SO	ERA
1986	Chicago Cubs	2	4	6	5	1	0	31.0	11	20	5.52
1987	Chicago Cubs	6	14	30	27	1	0	155.2	74	101	5.61
1988	Chicago Cubs	18	8	34	34	9	0	249.0	81	140	3.18
1989	Chicago Cubs	19	12	35	35	7	0	238.1	82	135	2.95
1990	Chicago Cubs	15	15	35	**35**	8	0	237.0	71	144	3.46
1991	Chicago Cubs	15	11	37	**37**	7	0	**263.0**	66	198	3.35
1992	Chicago Cubs	**20**	11	35	**35**	9	0	**268.0**	70	199	2.18
1993	Atlanta	20	10	36	**36**	8	0	**267.0**	52	197	**2.36**
1994	Atlanta	**16**	6	25	25	**10**	0	**202.0**	31	156	**1.56**
1995	Atlanta	**19**	2	28	28	**10**	0	**209.2**	23	181	**1.63**
1996	Atlanta	15	11	35	35	5	0	245.0	28	172	2.72
1997	Atlanta	19	4	33	33	5	0	232.2	20	177	2.20
1998	Atlanta	18	9	34	34	9	0	251.0	45	204	**2.22**
1999	Atlanta	19	9	33	33	4	0	219.1	37	136	3.57
2000	Atlanta	19	9	35	**35**	6	0	249.1	42	190	3.00
2001	Atlanta	17	11	34	34	3	0	233.0	27	173	3.05
2002	Atlanta	16	6	34	34	0	0	199.1	45	118	2.62
2003	Atlanta	16	11	36	36	1	0	218.1	33	124	3.96
Totals		**289**	**163**	**575**	**571**	**103**	**0**	**3968.2**	**838**	**2765**	**2.89**

Bold = Led league

Notes

>Eight-time All-Star (1988, 1992, 1994–1998, 2000);

>Pitched in postseason play 11 times, including three World Series (1995–1996, 1999) in which he posted a 2-3 record and a 2.09 ERA in five games;

>The first pitcher to win four consecutive Cy Young awards (1992–1995), he finished among the top five in the voting nine times;

>Earned 13 consecutive N.L. Gold Glove awards (1990–2002), and owns the record for most career putouts by a pitcher;

>His 2.54 ERA in the 1990s is the second-lowest ERA by a pitcher in a decade since the 1910s (Sandy Koufax had a 2.36 ERA in the 1960s);

>Owns the lowest ERA (2.15 from 1992–1998) over a seven-year span by any pitcher since World War II;

>First pitcher to post sub-1.70 ERA for consecutive seasons (1994–1995) since Walter Johnson in 1918–1919;

>Set an N.L. record for consecutive innings pitched without a walk (72.1) in 2001.

Juan Marichal (for more information, see pages 70–71)

Year	Team	W	L	G	GS	CG	SV	IP	BB	SO	ERA
1960	San Francisco	6	2	11	11	6	0	81.1	28	58	2.66
1961	San Francisco	13	10	29	27	9	0	185.0	48	124	3.89
1962	San Francisco	18	11	37	36	18	1	262.2	90	153	3.36
1963	San Francisco	**25**	8	41	40	18	0	**321.1**	61	248	2.41
1964	San Francisco	21	8	33	33	**22**	0	269.0	52	206	2.48
1965	San Francisco	22	13	39	37	24	1	295.1	46	240	2.13
1966	San Francisco	25	6	37	36	25	0	307.1	36	222	2.23
1967	San Francisco	14	10	26	26	18	0	202.1	42	166	2.76
1968	San Francisco	**26**	9	38	38	**30**	0	**326.0**	46	218	2.43
1969	San Francisco	21	11	37	36	27	0	299.2	54	205	**2.10**
1970	San Francisco	12	10	34	33	14	0	242.2	48	123	4.12
1971	San Francisco	18	11	37	37	18	0	279.0	56	159	2.94
1972	San Francisco	6	16	25	24	6	0	165.0	46	72	3.71
1973	San Francisco	11	15	34	32	9	0	207.1	37	87	3.82
1974	Boston	5	1	11	9	0	0	57.1	14	21	4.87
1975	Los Angeles	0	1	2	2	0	0	6.0	5	1	13.50
Totals		**243**	**142**	**471**	**457**	**244**	**2**	**3507.1**	**709**	**2303**	**2.89**

Bold = Led league

Notes
>Inducted into the Hall of Fame in 1983;
>Nine-time All-Star (1962–1969, 1971);
>Appeared in one World Series (1962), but pitched just four shutout innings before leaving Game 4 with a finger injury suffered while attempting to bunt;
>Hurled a no-hitter against Houston at Colt Stadium on June 15, 1963;
>Twice led the N.L. in shutouts (with 10 in 1965 and eight in 1969);
>A great control pitcher, Juan led the N.L. in fewest walks per nine innings four times (1965, 1966, 1969, 1973);
>His 30 complete games in 1968 were the most by any pitcher in the decade;
>Ranked among the top 10 in ERA seven consecutive seasons (1963–1969);
>Fired a one-hit shutout in his Major League debut against the Philadelphia Phillies on July 19, 1960;
>A back injury in 1970 brought on by a severe reaction to penicillin led to chronic arthritis and began Juan's decline;
>Pitched with an exaggerated leg kick, with his right hand nearly touching the ground as his left leg went high in the air before each delivery;
>The Giants signed him out of the Dominican Air Force when he was 19.

Dennis Martinez (for more information, see pages 14–15)

Year	Team	W	L	G	GS	CG	SV	IP	BB	SO	ERA
1976	Baltimore	1	2	4	2	1	0	27.2	8	18	2.60
1977	Baltimore	14	7	42	13	5	4	166.2	64	107	4.10
1978	Baltimore	16	11	40	38	15	0	276.1	93	142	3.52
1979	Baltimore	15	16	40	**39**	**18**	0	**292.1**	78	132	3.66
1980	Baltimore	6	4	25	12	2	1	99.2	44	42	3.97
1981	Baltimore	**14**	5	25	24	9	0	179.0	62	88	3.32
1982	Baltimore	16	12	40	39	10	0	252.0	87	111	4.21
1983	Baltimore	7	16	32	25	4	0	153.0	45	71	5.53
1984	Baltimore	6	9	34	20	2	0	141.2	37	77	5.02
1985	Baltimore	13	11	33	31	3	0	180.0	63	68	5.15
1986	Baltimore	0	0	4	0	0	0	6.2	2	2	6.75
1986	Montreal	3	6	19	15	1	0	98.0	28	63	4.59
1987	Montreal	11	4	22	22	2	0	144.2	40	84	3.30
1988	Montreal	15	13	34	34	9	0	235.1	55	120	2.72
1989	Montreal	16	7	34	33	5	0	232.0	49	142	3.18
1990	Montreal	10	11	32	32	7	0	226.0	49	156	2.95
1991	Montreal	14	11	31	31	**9**	0	222.0	62	123	**2.39**
1992	Montreal	16	11	32	32	6	0	226.1	60	147	2.47
1993	Montreal	15	9	35	34	2	1	224.2	64	138	3.85
1994	Cleveland	11	6	24	24	7	0	176.2	44	92	3.52
1995	Cleveland	12	5	28	28	3	0	187.0	46	99	3.08
1996	Cleveland	9	6	20	20	1	0	112.0	37	48	4.50
1997	Seattle	1	5	9	9	0	0	49.0	29	17	7.71
1998	Atlanta	4	6	53	5	1	2	91.0	19	62	4.45
Totals		**245**	**193**	**692**	**562**	**122**	**8**	**3999.2**	**1165**	**2149**	**3.70**

Bold = Led league

Notes

>Four-time All-Star (1990–1992, 1995);
>Appeared in two World Series (1979, 1995), though he did not win a game in four appearances, two of them starts;
>His perfect game against Los Angeles at Dodger Stadium on July 28, 1991 was the twelfth in baseball history.

Pedro Martinez (for more information, see pages 16–17)

Year	Team	W	L	G	GS	CG	SV	IP	BB	SO	ERA
1992	Los Angeles	0	1	2	1	0	0	8.0	1	8	2.25
1993	Los Angeles	10	5	65	2	0	2	107.0	57	119	2.61
1994	Montreal	11	5	24	23	1	1	144.2	45	142	3.42
1995	Montreal	14	10	3	30	2	0	194.2	66	174	3.51
1996	Montreal	13	10	33	33	4	0	216.2	70	222	3.70
1997	Montreal	17	8	31	31	**13**	0	241.1	67	305	**1.90**
1998	Boston	19	7	33	33	3	0	233.2	67	251	2.89
1999	Boston	**23**	4	31	29	5	0	213.1	37	**313**	2.07
2000	Boston	18	6	29	29	7	0	217.0	32	**284**	**1.74**
2001	Boston	7	3	18	18	1	0	116.2	25	163	2.39
2002	Boston	20	4	30	30	2	0	199.1	40	**239**	2.26
2003	Boston	14	4	29	29	3	0	186.2	47	206	2.22
Totals		**166**	**67**	**355**	**288**	**41**	**3**	**2079.0**	**554**	**2426**	**2.58**

Bold = Led league

Notes
>Six-time All-Star (1996–2000, 2002);
>Pitched in postseason three times, posting a 4-1 record in 8 games with a 3.10 ERA and 54 strikeouts in 52.1 innings;
>Won three Cy Young Awards (National League 1997, American League 1999 and 2000), becoming just the third pitcher to win the award in each league (joining Gaylord Perry and Randy Johnson);
>1999 American League pitching Triple Crown winner (wins, ERA, and strikeouts);
>Owns the highest career winning percentage (.712) for any pitcher with more than 200 decisions;
>Set single-season record for lowest batting average against (.167 in 2000);
>In 2000, his ERA (1.74) was almost 2.00 runs better than the runner-up in the American League (Roger Clemens, 3.70) and the American League average ERA in 2000 was 4.97;
>In 1997, he became the first right-hander with 300 strikeouts and an ERA under 2.00 in a season since Walter Johnson (1912);
>Joined Randy Johnson as the only pitcher with 300-strikeout seasons in each league, and in 1999 became the first pitcher with seven consecutive 10-strikeout games since Nolan Ryan in 1977;
>Traded by Los Angeles to Montreal for second baseman Delino Deshields—a deal still lamented by Dodgers fans ten years later—because Los Angeles feared the small-statured Martinez wouldn't be durable enough to be a full-time starter.

Christy Mathewson (for more information, see pages 96–97)

Year	Team	W	L	G	GS	CG	SV	IP	BB	SO	ERA
1900	N.Y. Giants	0	3	6	1	1	0	33.2	20	15	5.08
1901	N.Y. Giants	20	17	40	38	36	0	336.0	97	221	2.41
1902	N.Y. Giants	14	17	34	32	29	0	276.2	73	159	2.11
1903	N.Y. Giants	30	13	45	42	37	2	366.1	100	**267**	2.26
1904	N.Y. Giants	33	12	48	**46**	33	1	367.2	78	**212**	2.03
1905	N.Y. Giants	**31**	9	43	37	32	3	338.2	64	**206**	**1.28**
1906	N.Y. Giants	22	12	38	35	22	1	266.2	77	128	2.97
1907	N.Y. Giants	**24**	12	41	36	31	2	315.0	53	**178**	2.00
1908	N.Y. Giants	**37**	11	**56**	**44**	**34**	**5**	390.2	42	259	1.43
1909	N.Y. Giants	25	6	37	33	26	2	275.1	36	149	**1.14**
1910	N.Y. Giants	**27**	9	38	35	**27**	0	318.1	60	184	1.89
1911	N.Y. Giants	26	13	45	37	29	3	307.0	38	141	**1.99**
1912	N.Y. Giants	23	12	43	34	27	4	310.0	34	134	2.12
1913	N.Y. Giants	25	11	40	35	25	2	306.0	21	93	**2.06**
1914	N.Y. Giants	24	13	41	35	29	2	312.0	23	80	3.00
1915	N.Y. Giants	8	14	27	24	11	0	186.0	20	57	3.58
1916	N.Y. Giants	3	4	12	6	4	2	65.2	7	16	2.33
1916	Cincinnati	1	0	1	1	1	0	9.0	1	3	8.00
Totals		**373**	**188**	**635**	**551**	**434**	**28**	**4780.2**	**844**	**2502**	**2.13**

Bold = Led league

Notes

>One of five charter members elected to the Hall of Fame (1936);
>Pitched in four World Series (1905, 1911–1913), posting a 5-5 record and 1.06 ERA, completing 10 of 11 starts;
>Only pitcher to hurl 3 shutouts in a single World Series (1905)—and he did it in a span of six days;
>Two-time National League pitching Triple Crown winner (led in wins, ERA, and strikeouts in 1905 and 1908);
>Established post-1900 record for most 30-win seasons (four);
>Ranks in the top ten all-time in: wins (tied for third), shutouts (79, third), and ERA (eighth);
>Finished in the top four in the National League in wins eleven consecutive seasons (1903–1913);
>Twice won a National League-record tying 9 games in one month;
>His best pitch was a "fadeaway," which today is called a "screwball."

Jack Morris (for more information, see pages 98–99)

Year	Team	W	L	G	GS	CG	SV	IP	BB	SO	ERA
1977	Detroit	1	1	7	6	1	0	45.2	23	28	3.74
1978	Detroit	3	5	28	7	0	0	106.0	49	48	4.33
1979	Detroit	17	7	27	27	9	0	197.2	59	113	3.28
1980	Detroit	16	15	36	36	11	0	250.0	87	112	4.18
1981	Detroit	**14**	7	25	25	15	0	198.0	**78**	97	3.05
1982	Detroit	17	16	37	37	17	0	266.1	96	135	4.06
1983	Detroit	20	13	37	37	20	0	**293.2**	83	**232**	3.34
1984	Detroit	19	11	35	35	9	0	240.1	87	148	3.60
1985	Detroit	16	11	35	35	13	0	257.0	110	191	3.33
1986	Detroit	21	8	35	35	15	0	267.0	82	223	3.27
1987	Detroit	18	11	34	34	13	0	266.0	93	208	3.38
1988	Detroit	15	13	34	34	10	0	235.0	83	168	3.94
1989	Detroit	6	14	24	24	10	0	170.1	59	115	4.86
1990	Detroit	15	18	36	**36**	**11**	0	249.2	97	162	4.51
1991	Minnesota	18	12	35	**35**	10	0	246.2	92	163	3.43
1992	Toronto	**21**	6	34	34	6	0	240.2	80	132	4.04
1993	Toronto	7	12	27	27	4	0	152.2	65	103	6.19
1994	Detroit	10	6	23	23	1	0	141.1	67	100	5.60
Totals		**254**	**186**	**549**	**527**	**175**	**0**	**3824.0**	**1390**	**2478**	**3.90**

Bold = Led league

Notes
>All-Star selection in 1981, 1984–1985, 1987, and 1991;
>Pitched in seven postseason series, including three World Series (1984, 1991–1992) in which he posted a 4-2 record and a 2.96 ERA in seven games;
>Winningest pitcher of the 1980s (162 victories);
>Hurled a no-hitter against the White Sox on April 7, 1984 in Chicago;
>A durable starter, his 175 complete games was third only to Bert Blyleven and Nolan Ryan over the course of his career (1977–1994);
>Ranked among the top eight in the A.L. in complete games 10 times in 11 seasons from 1981–1991;
>Led the A.L. in shutouts (with 6) in 1986;
>A native of Minnesota, Morris signed a one-year contract with the Twins in 1991 and led them to their second World Series title.

Mark Mulder (for more information, see pages 18–19)

Year	Team	W	L	G	GS	CG	SV	IP	BB	SO	ERA
2000	Oakland	9	10	27	27	0	0	154.0	69	88	5.44
2001	Oakland	**21**	8	34	34	6	0	229.1	51	153	3.45
2002	Oakland	19	7	30	30	2	0	207.1	55	159	3.47
2003	Oakland	15	9	26	26	**9**	0	186.2	40	128	3.13
Totals		**64**	**34**	**117**	**117**	**17**	**0**	**777.1**	**215**	**528**	**3.77**

Bold = Led league

Notes

>Was selected to the All-Star Game in 2003;
>Has pitched in two postseason series, going 2-2 with a 2.25 ERA in four starts;
>Tied for the third-most victories (40) in the Major Leagues from 2001–2002, trailing only Randy Johnson and Curt Schilling (45 each);
>Led the A.L. with four shutouts in 2001;
>Also in 2001, was tied for second in the A.L. in complete games (six), tied for third in games started (34), tied for fifth in innings pitched (229.1), and ranked seventh in ERA (3.45);
>Finished strong in 2001, going 13-2 with a 2.87 ERA in his final 17 starts;
>In 2002, posted a 19-7 record despite spending 29 days on the disabled list;
>Tied for fourth in the A.L. in 2002 in wins (19), was third in pickoffs (7), seventh in opponents' batting average (.232), eighth in strikeouts (159), ninth in opponents' on-base percentage (.290), and 10th in ERA (3.47);
>In 2003, tied for the Major League lead in complete games (nine) despite missing the final six weeks of the season because of a stress fracture in his right femur;
>Completed five of six starts (including a stretch of three in a row) from April 24–May 23, 2003, posting a 5-1 record and a 1.21 ERA in 52 innings;
>Led all A.L. rookies in games started (27) and innings pitched (154) in 2000, and was second in wins (nine) and strikeouts (88);
>Posted career-high 11 strikeouts at Seattle on July 24, 2003, then matched the performance against Cleveland in his next start on July 29;
>Was the second pick of the June 1998 draft out of Michigan State, and was placed in Triple A to begin his professional career.

Mike Mussina (for more information, see pages 20–21)

Year	Team	W	L	G	GS	CG	SV	IP	BB	SO	ERA
1991	Baltimore	4	5	12	12	2	0	87.2	21	52	2.87
1992	Baltimore	18	5	32	32	8	0	241.0	48	130	2.54
1993	Baltimore	14	6	25	25	3	0	167.2	44	117	4.46
1994	Baltimore	16	5	24	24	3	0	176.1	42	99	3.06
1995	Baltimore	**19**	9	32	32	7	0	221.2	50	158	3.29
1996	Baltimore	19	11	36	**36**	4	0	243.1	69	204	4.81
1997	Baltimore	15	8	33	33	4	0	224.2	54	218	3.20
1998	Baltimore	13	10	29	29	4	0	206.1	41	175	3.49
1999	Baltimore	18	7	31	31	4	0	203.1	52	172	3.50
2000	Baltimore	11	15	34	34	6	0	**237.2**	46	210	3.79
2001	N.Y. Yankees	17	11	34	34	4	0	228.2	42	214	3.15
2002	N.Y. Yankees	18	10	33	33	2	0	215.2	48	182	4.05
2003	N.Y. Yankees	17	8	31	31	2	0	214.2	40	195	3.40
Totals		**199**	**110**	**386**	**386**	**53**	**0**	**2668.2**	**597**	**2126**	**3.53**

Bold = Led league

Notes
> Five-time All-Star (1992–1994, 1997, 1999);
> Pitched in five postseason series, including two World Series (2001, 2003) in which he posted an 1-1 record and 3.00 ERA with 23 strikeouts in 18 innings;
> Set ALCS record with 15 strikeouts at Cleveland (October 11, 1997), pitching just the first seven innings;
> Six-time American League Gold Glove award winner (1996–1999, 2001, 2003);
> Only pitcher to toss at least 200 innings in each of the past nine seasons;
> Ranked in the top six in American League Cy Young Award voting eight times and ranked in the top four in American League in ERA six times;
> Fourth-most victories (177) in last eleven seasons (1993–2003), trailing just Greg Maddux (194), Randy Johnson (181), and Tom Glavine (178);
> Finished in the top ten in the American League in strikeouts each of the past nine seasons;
> One of the best control pitchers in baseball, has ranked in the top ten in walks per innings pitched each of the past twelve seasons;
> Earned an economics degree from Stanford, finishing school in just 3½ years.

Don Newcombe (for more information, see pages 72–73)

Year	Team	W	L	G	GS	CG	SV	IP	BB	SO	ERA
1949	Brooklyn	17	8	38	31	19	1	244.1	73	149	3.17
1950	Brooklyn	19	11	40	35	20	3	267.1	75	130	3.70
1951	Brooklyn	20	9	40	36	18	0	272.0	91	**164**	3.28
1954	Brooklyn	9	8	29	25	6	0	144.1	49	82	4.55
1955	Brooklyn	20	5	34	31	17	0	233.2	38	143	3.20
1956	Brooklyn	**27**	7	38	36	18	0	268.0	46	139	3.06
1957	Brooklyn	11	12	28	28	12	0	198.2	33	90	3.49
1958	Los Angeles	0	6	11	8	1	0	34.1	8	16	7.86
1958	Cincinnati	7	7	20	18	7	1	133.1	28	53	3.85
1959	Cincinnati	13	8	30	29	17	1	222.0	27	100	3.16
1960	Cincinnati	4	6	16	15	1	0	82.2	14	36	4.57
1960	Cleveland	2	3	20	2	0	1	54.0	8	27	4.33
Totals		**149**	**90**	**344**	**294**	**136**	**7**	**2154.2**	**490**	**1129**	**3.56**

Bold = Led league

Notes

>Four-time All-Star (1949–1951, 1955);
>Pitched in three World Series (1949, 1955, 1956), posting an 0-4 record and 8.59 ERA in 5 games;
>1956 National League Cy Young and Most Valuable Player award winners;
>National League Rookie of the Year winner (1949);
>Only player ever to win Rookie of the Year, MVP, and Cy Young Awards;
>First African-American pitcher to win Rookie of the Year and Cy Young Awards;
>Led National League in shutouts as a rookie (5 in 1949);
>Hurled 32 consecutive scoreless innings as a rookie during the 1949 pennant race, which the Dodgers won by one game;
>A tremendous hitter, his .271 career average ranks ninth all-time among pitchers, and he hit a National League record (for pitchers) 7 homers in 1955, including two 2-homer games;
>Played first base in Japan after he retired from the major leagues;
>Missed 2½ seasons while serving in the military (1952–1954);
>Was the Dodgers' starting pitcher in Game Three of the 1951 National League playoffs, and put two runners on in the ninth inning, before Ralph Branca relieved him and allowed the famous home run by Bobby Thomson.

Hideo Nomo (for more information, see pages 22–23)

Year	Team	W	L	G	GS	CG	SV	IP	BB	SO	ERA
1995	Los Angeles	13	6	28	28	4	0	191.1	78	**236**	2.54
1996	Los Angeles	16	11	33	33	3	0	228.1	85	234	3.19
1997	Los Angeles	14	12	33	33	1	0	207.1	92	233	4.25
1998	Los Angeles	2	7	12	12	2	0	67.2	38	73	5.05
1998	N.Y. Mets	4	5	17	16	1	0	89.2	56	94	4.82
1999	Milwaukee	12	8	28	28	0	0	176.1	78	161	4.54
2000	Detroit	8	12	32	31	1	0	190.0	89	181	4.74
2001	Boston	13	10	33	33	2	0	198.0	**96**	**220**	4.50
2002	Los Angeles	16	6	34	34	0	0	220.1	101	193	3.39
2003	Los Angeles	16	13	33	33	2	0	218.1	98	177	3.09
Totals		**114**	**90**	**283**	**281**	**16**	**0**	**1787.1**	**811**	**1802**	**3.85**

Bold = Led league

Notes
>N.L. All-Star in 1995 who was the first rookie pitcher for either league to start in the game since Fernando Valenzuela in 1981;
>Pitched in two postseason series, making two starts;
>1995 N.L. Rookie of the Year;
>Hurled the only no-hitter tossed in Coors Field history on September 17, 1996;
>His second career no-hitter was at Baltimore on April 4, 2001 (the earliest date in history that a no-hitter was tossed), and it came in his first start for Boston (marking the first time a pitcher had thrown a no-hitter in his initial start with a club since Wilson Alvarez for the White Sox in 1991);
>Led the N.L. in strikeouts (236) and shutouts (three), and led the Major Leagues in batting average against (.182) in 1995;
>Set Dodgers rookie record with 16 strikeouts at Pittsburgh on June 14, 1995, and struck out a career-high 17 batters against Florida on April 13, 1997;
>Established a Dodgers record for strikeouts in a four-game span (50), breaking the mark held by Sandy Koufax;
>Played five seasons in Japan, leading the league in wins four times, in strikeouts three times, and ERA once while completing nearly 60 percent of his starts;
>As a rookie in Japan in 1990, he won pitching's unofficial Triple Crown (leading his league in wins, ERA, and strikeouts) and was honored with the equivalent of the Japanese League MVP, Cy Young, and Rookie of the Year awards.

Satchel Paige (for more information, see pages 74–75)

Year	Team	W	L	G	GS	CG	SV	IP	BB	SO	ERA
1948	Cleveland	6	1	21	7	3	1	72.2	22	43	2.48
1949	Cleveland	4	7	31	5	1	5	83.0	33	54	3.04
1951	St. L. Browns	3	4	23	3	0	5	62.0	29	48	4.79
1952	St. L. Browns	12	10	46	6	3	10	138.0	57	91	3.07
1953	St. L. Browns	3	9	57	4	0	11	117.1	39	51	3.53
1965	K.C. Athletics	0	0	1	1	0	0	3.0	0	1	0.00
Totals		**28**	**31**	**179**	**26**	**7**	**32**	**476.0**	**183**	**290**	**3.29**

Notes

> In 1971, became the first man elected to the Hall of Fame by the Committee on Negro Leagues;

> Two-time All-Star (1952–1953) and the oldest All-Star ever (47 in 1953);

> Pitched in one World Series (1948), retiring both batters he faced in Game 5;

> Pitched professionally, primarily in the Negro Leagues, from 1924–1959, and appeared in one game in 1965;

> First African-American pitcher in A.L. history;

> Hurled two shutouts in 1948 at age 42, including one in just his second start;

> In 1952, at age 46, finished with 12 wins, including an A.L.-leading eight victories in relief, and finished second in the league in saves (10);

> In 1953, was fourth in the A.L. in saves (11);

> Best documented season was 1933, when he posted a 31-4 record for the Pittsburgh Crawfords, won 21 consecutive games, and registered 62 consecutive scoreless innings;

> Struck out 22 Major League hitters in an exhibition game in 1930;

> During his exhibition games, he became famous for calling in the outfielders before the inning started and then striking out the side;

> Joe DiMaggio called Satchel "the best and fastest pitcher I've ever faced.";

> Satchel delivered pitches with a windmill windup in which he would rotate his right arm in a full circle before throwing the pitch, or with a "hesitation," in which he would stop in the middle of his windup before continuing;

Jim Palmer (for more information, see pages 24–25)

Year	Team	W	L	G	GS	CG	SV	IP	BB	SO	ERA
1965	Baltimore	5	4	27	6	0	1	92.0	56	75	3.72
1966	Baltimore	15	10	30	30	6	0	208.1	91	147	3.46
1967	Baltimore	3	1	9	9	2	0	49.0	20	23	2.94
1969	Baltimore	16	4	26	23	11	0	181.0	64	123	2.34
1970	Baltimore	20	10	39	39	17	0	**305.0**	100	199	2.71
1971	Baltimore	20	9	37	37	20	0	282.0	106	184	2.68
1972	Baltimore	21	10	36	36	18	0	274.1	70	184	2.07
1973	Baltimore	22	9	38	37	19	1	296.1	113	158	**2.40**
1974	Baltimore	7	12	26	26	6	0	178.2	69	84	3.27
1975	Baltimore	**23**	11	39	38	25	1	323.0	80	193	**2.09**
1976	Baltimore	**22**	13	40	**40**	23	0	**315.0**	84	159	2.51
1977	Baltimore	**20**	11	39	**39**	22	0	**319.0**	99	193	2.91
1978	Baltimore	21	12	38	38	19	0	**296.0**	97	138	2.46
1979	Baltimore	10	6	23	22	7	0	155.2	43	67	3.30
1980	Baltimore	16	10	34	33	4	0	224.0	74	109	3.98
1981	Baltimore	7	8	22	22	5	0	127.1	46	35	3.75
1982	Baltimore	15	5	36	32	8	1	227.0	63	103	3.13
1983	Baltimore	5	4	14	11	0	0	76.2	19	34	4.23
1984	Baltimore	0	3	5	3	0	0	17.2	17	4	9.17
Totals		**268**	**152**	**558**	**521**	**211**	**4**	**3948.0**	**1311**	**2212**	**2.86**

Bold = Led league

Notes
>Six-time All-Star (1970–1972, 1975, 1977–1978);
>Pitched in 12 postseason series, including six World Series (1966, 1969–1971, 1979, 1983) in which he posted a 4-2 record and a 3.20 ERA in nine games;
>Won the A.L. Cy Young award in 1973, 1975, and 1976);
>Four-time A.L. Gold Glove award winner (1976–1979);
>Jim, Walter Johnson, and Lefty Grove are the only A.L. pitchers to win at least 20 games eight times;
>Hurled a no-hitter against Oakland on August 13, 1969;
>Last A.L. pitcher to toss 10 shutouts in a season (1975);
>Missed most of 1967, and all of the 1968 season, because of arm, shoulder, and back injuries, and was unprotected in the expansion draft, but was not taken.

Troy Percival (for more information, see pages 108–109)

Year	Team	W	L	G	GS	CG	SV	IP	BB	SO	ERA
1995	California	3	2	62	0	0	3	74.0	26	94	1.95
1996	California	0	2	62	0	0	36	74.0	31	100	2.31
1997	Anaheim	5	5	55	0	0	27	52.0	22	72	3.46
1998	Anaheim	2	7	67	0	0	42	66.2	37	87	3.65
1999	Anaheim	4	6	60	0	0	31	57.0	22	58	3.79
2000	Anaheim	5	5	54	0	0	32	50.0	30	49	4.50
2001	Anaheim	4	2	57	0	0	39	57.2	18	71	2.65
2002	Anaheim	4	1	58	0	0	40	56.1	25	68	1.92
2003	Anaheim	0	5	52	0	0	33	49.1	23	48	3.47
Totals		**27**	**35**	**527**	**0**	**0**	**283**	**537.0**	**234**	**647**	**3.00**

Bold = Led league

Notes

>Four-time All-Star (1996, 1998–1999, 2001);

>Pitched in three postseason series, including one World Series (2002) in which he was 3-for-3 in save chances and had an ERA of 3.00;

>Tied the Major League record in 2002 for most saves in a single postseason (7);

>Has played his entire big-league career with the Angels (they changed their name from "California" to "Anaheim" prior to the 1997 season);

>Only pitcher to appear in at least 50 games and post at least 25 saves each season since 1996;

>Ranked among the top six in the A.L. in saves seven times in eight seasons from 1996–2003;

>One of just nine pitchers to have appeared in at least 50 games in each of the past eight seasons;

>Owns career rate of 10.84 strikeouts per nine innings;

>Angels record holder for saves and games pitched;

>Was a standout catcher in college at UC Riverside and played one season as a catcher in the minors, hitting just .203 with five RBI in 79 at-bats, before being converted to the mound in 1991;

>In his first season as a pitcher, led the Northwest (Rookie) League with 12 saves while posting a 1.41 ERA and striking out 63 batters in 38.1 innings.

Andy Pettitte (for more information, see pages 26–27)

Year	Team	W	L	G	GS	CG	SV	IP	BB	SO	ERA
1995	N.Y. Yankees	12	9	31	26	3	0	175.0	63	114	4.17
1996	N.Y. Yankees	**21**	8	35	34	2	0	221.0	72	162	3.87
1997	N.Y. Yankees	18	7	35	**35**	4	0	240.1	65	166	2.88
1998	N.Y. Yankees	16	11	33	32	5	0	216.1	87	146	4.24
1999	N.Y. Yankees	14	11	31	31	0	0	191.2	89	121	4.70
2000	N.Y. Yankees	19	9	32	32	3	0	204.2	80	125	4.35
2001	N.Y. Yankees	15	10	31	31	2	0	200.2	41	164	3.99
2002	N.Y. Yankees	13	5	22	22	3	0	134.2	32	97	3.27
2003	N.Y. Yankees	21	8	33	33	1	0	208.1	50	180	4.02
Totals		**149**	**78**	**283**	**276**	**23**	**0**	**1792.2**	**579**	**1275**	**3.94**

Bold = Led league

Notes

> Two-time All-Star (1996, 2001);

> Pitched in postseason nine times, including six World Series (1996, 1998, 1999, 2000, 2001, 2003) in which he posted a 3-4 record and 3.90 ERA;

> Was the 2001 ALCS Most Valuable Player when he was 2-0 with a 2.51 ERA in 2 starts;

> Tied for first all-time in postseason victories (13) with John Smoltz;

> Finished in the top five in American League Cy Young Award voting three times (second in 1996, fifth in 1997, and fourth in 2000);

> First pitcher in almost 70 years to win at least 12 games in each of his first nine full seasons (Stan Coveleski, 1916–1926);

> Tied for second in the American League in wins (21) in 2003, and ranked sixth in the league in winning percentage (.724);

> Posted career-high 7.78 strikeout per-nine inning ratio (2003);

> Allowed just 7 home runs in 240.1 innings pitched (1997);

> With maybe the best move in baseball, leads the majors in pickoffs (67) during the past nine seasons;

> In Yankees storied annals, ranks in the top nine in victories and strikeouts;

> Has memorable mound presence, as he wears his cap tight on his head, just above his eyes, and then looks in for the catcher's sign with his glove shielding his nose, thus allowing the hitter to only see his eyes.

Mark Prior
(for more information, see pages 28–29)

Year	Team	W	L	G	GS	CG	SV	IP	BB	SO	ERA
2002	Chicago Cubs	6	6	19	19	1	0	116.2	38	147	3.32
2003	Chicago Cubs	18	6	30	30	3	0	211.1	50	245	2.43
Totals		**24**	**12**	**49**	**49**	**4**	**0**	**328.0**	**88**	**392**	**2.74**

Notes

>Selected to one All-Star Game (2003);

>Pitched in one postseason, posting a 2-1 record in 3 games with a 2.31 ERA and 18 strikeouts in 23 innings;

>Reached double-digits in strikeouts in three of his first five starts, marking the first rookie to achieve that feat since Fernando Valenzuela in 1981;

>In 2003, had eight games with double-digit strikeouts, including each of his last three appearances as the Cubs won the National League Central by one game;

>Has 14 double-digit strikeout games in 49 career starts (29 percent);

>Struck out 10 Pirates in his major-league debut, the most by a Cubs pitcher since 1969 (May 22, 2002);

>Registered a career-high 16 strikeouts against Milwaukee (June 26, 2002);

>Tied club record with 7 consecutive strikeouts against Houston on August 15, 2002 (joining Jamie Moyer and Kerry Wood);

>Was injured while running the bases when he flipped over Braves second baseman Marcus Giles and landed on his own shoulder (July 11, 2003);

>Returned from disabled list on August 5, 2003, to win 10 of his final 11 games, posting a 1.52 ERA and striking out 95 in 82.2 innings while allowing just 83 baserunners;

>Finished strong in 2002, also, striking out 61 and allowing just 8 walks in 43.2 innings covering his final seven starts;

>Was drafted in the first round in 2001, but did not play professionally until 2002;

>Made just nine minor-league starts, including six at West Tenn (Double A) in which he was 5-2 with a 2.34 ERA, and struck out the first 6 batters he faced in his first-ever professional game;

>In three starts at Triple A Iowa, went 1-1 with a 1.65 ERA, including striking out the side on 10 pitches in his first inning with Iowa.

Mariano Rivera (for more information, see pages 110–111)

Year	Team	W	L	G	GS	CG	SV	IP	BB	SO	ERA
1995	N.Y. Yankees	5	3	19	10	0	0	67.0	30	51	5.51
1996	N.Y. Yankees	8	3	61	0	0	5	107.2	34	130	2.09
1997	N.Y. Yankees	6	4	66	0	0	43	71.2	20	68	1.88
1998	N.Y. Yankees	3	0	54	0	0	36	61.1	17	36	1.91
1999	N.Y. Yankees	4	3	66	0	0	**45**	69.0	18	52	1.83
2000	N.Y. Yankees	7	4	66	0	0	36	75.2	25	58	2.85
2001	N.Y. Yankees	4	6	71	0	0	**50**	80.2	12	83	2.34
2002	N.Y. Yankees	1	4	45	0	0	28	46.0	11	41	2.74
2003	N.Y. Yankees	5	2	64	0	0	40	70.2	10	63	1.66
Totals		**43**	**29**	**512**	**10**	**0**	**283**	**649.2**	**177**	**582**	**2.49**

Bold = Led league

Notes
> Five-time All-Star (1997, 1999–2002);
> Pitched in nine postseason series, including six World Series (1996, 1998–2001, 2003) in which he posted a 2-1 record and a World Series-record 9 saves; was selected 1999 World Series MVP award when he was 1-0 with 2 saves and 0.00 ERA in 3 games;
> Hurled 32.1 consecutive scoreless innings in the postseason from 1997–2000;
> Started 66 percent of his 102 minor-league games, highlighted by hurling seven-inning and five-inning no-hitters, and started 10 games as a rookie in 1995 before his impressive performance in the 1995 postseason, when he pitched 5.1 innings and allowed 4 baserunners, 8 strikeouts, and no runs, convinced the Yankees to put him in the bullpen on a permanent basis;
> Served as set-up man for John Wetteland prior to taking over closer role in 1997;
> Ranked in the top seven in the American League in saves each of the past seven seasons (1997–2003);
> Yankees all-time leader in saves;
> Best pitch is a cut-fastball, which darts in on the hands of right-handed hitters;
> Born in Panama and was not signed by Yankees until age 20, and did not reach the majors until age 25.

Nolan Ryan (for more information, see pages 50–51)

Year	Team	W	L	G	GS	CG	SV	IP	BB	SO	ERA
1966	N.Y. Mets	0	1	2	1	0	0	3.0	3	6	15.00
1968	N.Y. Mets	6	9	21	18	3	0	134.0	75	133	3.09
1969	N.Y. Mets	6	3	25	10	2	1	89.1	53	92	3.53
1970	N.Y. Mets	7	11	27	19	5	1	131.2	97	125	3.42
1971	N.Y. Mets	10	14	30	26	3	0	152.0	116	137	3.97
1972	California	19	16	39	39	20	0	284.0	**157**	**329**	2.28
1973	California	21	16	41	39	26	1	326.0	**162**	**383**	2.87
1974	California	22	16	42	41	26	0	**332.2**	**202**	367	2.89
1975	California	14	12	28	28	10	0	198.0	132	186	3.45
1976	California	17	**18**	39	39	21	0	284.1	**183**	**327**	3.36
1977	California	19	16	37	37	**22**	0	299.0	**204**	**341**	2.77
1978	California	10	13	31	31	14	0	234.2	**148**	**260**	3.72
1979	California	16	14	34	34	17	0	222.2	114	**223**	3.60
1980	Houston	11	10	35	35	4	0	233.2	**98**	200	3.35
1981	Houston	11	5	21	21	5	0	149.0	68	140	**1.69**
1982	Houston	16	12	35	35	10	0	250.1	**109**	245	3.16
1983	Houston	14	9	29	29	5	0	196.1	101	183	2.98
1984	Houston	12	11	30	30	5	0	183.2	69	197	3.04
1985	Houston	10	12	35	35	4	0	232.0	95	209	3.80
1986	Houston	12	8	30	30	1	0	178.0	82	194	3.34
1987	Houston	8	16	34	34	0	0	211.2	87	**270**	**2.76**
1988	Houston	12	11	33	33	4	0	220.0	87	**228**	3.52
1989	Texas	16	10	32	32	6	0	239.1	98	**301**	3.20
1990	Texas	13	9	30	30	5	0	204.0	74	**232**	3.44
1991	Texas	12	6	27	27	2	0	173.0	72	203	2.91
1992	Texas	5	9	27	27	2	0	157.1	69	157	3.72
1993	Texas	5	5	13	13	0	0	66.1	40	46	4.88
Totals		**324**	**292**	**807**	**773**	**222**	**3**	**5386.0**	**2795**	**5714**	**3.19**

Bold = Led league

Notes
> First-ballot Hall of Fame inductee (1999);
> Eight-time All-Star (1972, 1973, 1975, 1977, 1979, 1981, 1985, 1989);
> Pitched in six postseason series, including one World Series (1969), in which he recorded 1 save in 2.1 innings and struck out 3 in his only appearance;
> Ranks in the top ten all-time in: strikeouts (first, nearly 1,600 more than second place), walks (first), starts (second), innings (fifth), and shutouts (seventh, 61).

Curt Schilling (for more information, see pages 52–53)

Year	Team	W	L	G	GS	CG	SV	IP	BB	SO	ERA
1988	Baltimore	0	3	4	4	0	0	14.2	10	4	9.82
1989	Baltimore	0	1	5	1	0	0	8.2	3	6	6.23
1990	Baltimore	1	2	35	0	0	3	46.0	19	32	2.54
1991	Houston	3	5	56	0	0	8	75.2	39	71	3.81
1992	Philadelphia	14	11	42	26	10	2	226.1	59	147	2.35
1993	Philadelphia	16	7	34	34	7	0	235.1	57	186	4.02
1994	Philadelphia	2	8	13	13	1	0	82.1	28	58	4.48
1995	Philadelphia	7	5	17	17	1	0	116.0	26	114	3.57
1996	Philadelphia	9	10	26	26	**8**	0	183.1	50	182	3.19
1997	Philadelphia	17	11	35	**35**	7	0	254.1	58	**319**	2.97
1998	Philadelphia	15	14	35	**35**	**15**	0	**268.2**	61	**300**	3.25
1999	Philadelphia	15	6	24	24	8	0	180.1	44	152	3.54
2000	Philadelphia	6	6	16	16	**4**	0	112.2	32	96	3.91
2000	Arizona	5	6	13	13	**4**	0	97.2	13	72	3.69
2001	Arizona	**22**	6	35	**35**	6	0	**256.2**	39	293	2.98
2002	Arizona	23	7	36	35	5	0	259.1	33	316	3.23
2003	Arizona	8	9	24	24	3	0	168.0	32	194	2.95
Totals		**163**	**117**	**450**	**338**	**79**	**13**	**2586.0**	**603**	**2542**	**3.33**

Bold = Led league

Notes

>Five-time All-Star (1997–1999, 2001–2002);
>Pitched in six postseason series, including two World Series (1993, 2001) in which he went 2-1 with a 2.45 ERA and 35 strikeouts in 36.2 innings;
>In the 2001 World Series, he was 1-0 with a 1.69 ERA in three starts and shared MVP honors with teammate Randy Johnson;
>Hurled record 48.1 postseason innings in 2001, going 4-0 with a 1.12 ERA;
>Also voted the 1993 NLCS Most Valuable Player with a 1.69 ERA and 19 strikeouts in 16 innings;
>Both he and Randy Johnson each won 45 games from 2001–2002, matching the most wins in a two-year span since Jim Palmer in 1975–1976;
>Combined with Randy Johnson to set a record for most strikeouts by a pair of teammates in a season (665 in 2001, passing Nolan Ryan and Bill Singer, who had 624 for California in 1973);
>One of four pitchers to have at least three 300-strikeout seasons (1997–1998, 2001), and only the sixth pitcher to post consecutive 300-strikeout seasons.

Tom Seaver (for more information, see pages 54–55)

Year	Team	W	L	G	GS	CG	SV	IP	BB	SO	ERA
1967	N.Y. Mets	16	13	35	34	18	0	251.0	78	170	2.76
1968	N.Y. Mets	16	12	36	35	14	1	277.2	48	205	2.20
1969	N.Y. Mets	**25**	7	36	35	18	0	273.1	82	208	2.21
1970	N.Y. Mets	18	12	37	36	19	0	290.2	83	**283**	**2.82**
1971	N.Y. Mets	20	10	36	35	21	0	286.1	61	**289**	**1.76**
1972	N.Y. Mets	21	12	35	35	13	0	262.0	77	249	2.92
1973	N.Y. Mets	19	10	36	36	**18**	0	290.0	64	**251**	**2.08**
1974	N.Y. Mets	11	11	32	32	12	0	236.0	75	201	3.20
1975	N.Y. Mets	**22**	9	36	36	15	0	280.1	88	**243**	2.38
1976	N.Y. Mets	14	11	35	34	13	0	271.0	77	**235**	2.59
1977	N.Y. Mets	7	3	13	13	5	0	96.0	28	72	3.00
1977	Cincinnati	14	3	20	20	14	0	165.1	38	124	2.34
1978	Cincinnati	16	14	36	36	8	0	259.2	89	226	2.88
1979	Cincinnati	16	6	32	32	9	0	215.0	61	131	3.14
1980	Cincinnati	10	8	26	26	5	0	168.0	59	101	3.64
1981	Cincinnati	**14**	2	23	23	6	0	166.1	66	87	2.54
1982	Cincinnati	5	13	21	21	0	0	111.1	44	62	5.50
1983	N.Y. Mets	9	14	34	34	5	0	231.0	86	135	3.55
1984	Chi. White Sox	15	11	34	33	10	0	236.2	61	131	3.95
1985	Chi. White Sox	16	11	35	33	6	0	238.2	69	134	3.17
1986	Chi. White Sox	2	6	12	12	1	0	72.0	27	31	4.38
1986	Boston	5	7	16	16	1	0	104.1	29	72	3.80
Totals		**311**	**205**	**656**	**647**	**231**	**1**	**4782.2**	**1390**	**3640**	**2.86**

Bold = Led league

Notes

> First-ballot Hall of Fame inductee in 1992;
> Was selected to the All-Star Game 12 times (1967–1973, 1975–1978, 1981);
> Pitched in five postseason series, including two World Series (1969 and 1973) in which he posted a 1-2 record and had a 2.70 ERA;
> Three-time N.L. Cy Young award winner (1969, 1973, 1975);
> N.L. Rookie of the Year award recipient in 1967;
> Struck out a record 10 consecutive hitters on April 22, 1970 against San Diego (he struck out 19 in all that game to equal the Major League record at the time);
> Hurled a no-hitter against St. Louis on June 16, 1978;
> Is tied for seventh all-time with 61 shutouts.

Lee Smith (for more information, see pages 112–113)

Year	Team	W	L	G	GS	CG	SV	IP	BB	SO	ERA
1980	Chicago Cubs	2	0	18	0	0	0	21.2	14	17	2.91
1981	Chicago Cubs	3	6	40	1	0	1	66.2	31	50	3.51
1982	Chicago Cubs	2	5	72	5	0	17	117.0	37	99	2.69
1983	Chicago Cubs	4	10	66	0	0	**29**	103.1	41	91	1.65
1984	Chicago Cubs	9	7	69	0	0	33	101.0	35	86	3.65
1985	Chicago Cubs	7	4	65	0	0	33	97.2	32	112	3.04
1986	Chicago Cubs	9	9	66	0	0	31	90.1	42	93	3.09
1987	Chicago Cubs	4	10	62	0	0	36	83.2	32	96	3.12
1988	Boston	4	5	64	0	0	29	83.2	37	96	2.80
1989	Boston	6	1	64	0	0	25	70.2	33	96	3.57
1990	Boston	2	1	11	0	0	4	14.1	9	17	1.88
1990	St. Louis	3	4	53	0	0	27	68.2	20	70	2.10
1991	St. Louis	6	3	67	0	0	**47**	73.0	13	67	2.34
1992	St. Louis	4	9	70	0	0	**43**	75.0	26	60	3.12
1993	St. Louis	2	4	55	0	0	43	50.0	9	49	4.50
1993	N.Y. Yankees	0	0	8	0	0	3	8.0	5	11	0.00
1994	Baltimore	1	4	41	0	0	**33**	38.1	11	42	3.29
1995	California	0	5	52	0	0	37	49.1	25	43	3.47
1996	California	0	0	11	0	0	0	11.0	3	6	2.45
1996	Cincinnati	3	4	43	0	0	2	44.1	23	35	4.06
1997	Montreal	0	1	25	0	0	5	21.2	8	15	5.82
Totals		**71**	**92**	**1022**	**6**	**0**	**478**	**1289.1**	**486**	**1251**	**3.03**

Bold = Led league

Notes
> Seven-time All-Star (1983, 1987, 1991–1995);
> Finished second in the N.L. Cy Young Award voting (1991);
> All-time leader in saves (478), and ranks seventh in games (1,022);
> From 1991–1993, he became the second pitcher with three consecutive 40-save seasons (following Dennis Eckersley);
> Ranked in the top nine in saves in 14 consecutive seasons (1982–1995);
> Used to walk from the clubhouse to the bullpen during the seventh-inning stretch of a game
> His walk from the bullpen to the mound was perhaps the slowest in history.